CHASING TRAINS

VOLUME 3   MAKING TRACKS

Martin Buck

FREIGHTMASTER

PUBLISHING

CONTENTS

Published by :

Freightmaster Publishing
158 Overbrook
SWINDON
SN3 6AY

www.freightmasterpublishing.co.uk

First published : November 2020

ISBN : 978-0-9933129-5-3

Printed By :

Stephens & George
Goat Mill Road
Dowlais
MERTHYR TYDFIL
CF48 3TD

Design : Martin Buck, unless otherwise accredited.
& Images

How CT 3 Came About

CT3 sounds more like a proposed new railway route, but I can assure you it is not, just the third book in what has now become a 'trilogy' in the "Chasing Trains" series. In fact, the 'trilogy' nearly did not come about at all, merely by chance following a discussion with my friend Peter, with whom I used to work with at a leading life assurance company in Swindon more than 30 years ago.

Having mentioned that I had decided to compile a sequel, his response was:

"sounds good, but why not a trilogy"

Having mulled the idea around in my head, I felt this was a really good idea. So, thank you, Peter.

I must confess, I always intended to do a sequel, irrespective of its success but, when sales exceeded my wildest expectations, a sequel became a reality. So, I started work and quickly discovered that I had already compiled some 400 pages and so the sequel had turned in to a trilogy by default.

The original book took some 15 years to complete, primarily due to other circumstances, but the second and third titles were completed in a matter of months. Between March - July 2020, the country was in 'lockdown' and people were confined to their home as a result of a Covid-19 virus pandemic sweeping the world. During these restrictions, I was able to work pretty well uninterrupted on these titles and so Volume two and Volume three is the result.

About Chasing Trains 3

This edition is completely different in concept, to reflect how my railway interests changed, with a greater emphasis on travelling over routes and branch lines I had not previously visited. I found this really interesting although the only downside was the majority were DMU/EMU operation and not loco-hauled. With this in mind, I have recounted some of the more memorable trips.

One major change where I live (Swindon) is the electrification of the Great Western Main Line between London Paddington - Cardiff Central and Chippenham; Bath and Bristol Temple Meads being unelectrified. The main line boasted many great photographic locations, but many of these have disappeared since the wires went up. I considered this a new challenge and I set out to illustrate how electrification has affected locations in around Swindon; the results are shown from Page 156 onwards. I hope I have been able to demonstrate that it is still possible to photograph 'under the wires'.

Finally, a few thanks would not go amiss; I would like to thank each of you who have purchased a copy of "Chasing Trains", not forgetting of course, my wife, Joanne, who has always supported my endeavours and proof read the manuscripts, a painstaking but invaluable task.

Hope you enjoy.

Martin Buck

2020

60 Years and Still Going Strong

The Class 37 has become a familiar sight on many parts of the British Rail network and are well liked by enthusiasts, who have christened them *"Tractors"* due to the agricultural sound made by the loco's diesel engine.

I thought I would mark the occasion of their 60th birthday by looking out a small selection of photographs (in addition to those seen in *'Chasing Trains 2'*), although I must confess to having fewer than I would have liked. However ....

Despite all members of the class now being over 60 years old, as at 1st April 2020, 40 locos were still in active service on the main line with nearly the same number preserved, many of which still being mainline registered. Although passenger activity is now pretty well eliminated, the Class undertake a variety of freight duties, most notably with freight operators DRS and Colas Rail.

Historical Perspective

The Class 37 loco - aka English Electric Type 3 - was ordered by British Rail under the British Rail modernisation plan. They were numbered in two series;

Originally	D6600 - D6608	D6700 - D6999
Under TOPS	37301 - 37308	37119, then 37001 - 37299

Order	Year	No.	Batch	Built at:
CCL 1031	January 1959	42	D6700 - 41	Vulcan Foundry
CCM 1114	February 1960	37	D6742 - 68	Vulcan Foundry
			D6769 - 78	Robert Stephenson & Hawthorns
CCN 1239	April 1961	17	D6779 - 95	Robert Stephenson & Hawthorns
CCP 1267	December 1961	23	D6796 - 6818	Vulcan Foundry
CCP 1304	July 1962	100	D6819 - 28	Robert Stephenson & Hawthorns
			D6829 - 58	Vulcan Foundry
			D6859 - 68	Robert Stephenson & Hawthorns
			D6869 - 78	Vulcan Foundry
			D6879 - 98	Robert Stephenson & Hawthorns
			D6899 - 6918	Vulcan Foundry
CCR 1320	January 1964	20	D6919 - 38	Vulcan Foundry
CCS 1362	February 1964	70	D6939 - 99	Vulcan Foundry
			D6600 - 08	Vulcan Foundry

The 37s were designed for both passenger and freight work and many of the original locos were fitted with boilers for steam heating from new; D6700 - D6754, D6758, D6775, D6781 - D6818 and D6875 - D6892. With the withdrawal of many Type 2 locos in the 1980s, quite a few 37s were given a heavy overhaul to prolong their life. Some were fitted with electrical train heating (ETH) equipment in the 1980s to become the 37/4 sub-class and found work on passenger duties, such as:

- West Highland Line   (Fort William / Mallaig)
- Far North Lines   (Kyle of Lochalsh / Thurso / Wick)
- Welsh Marches line   (Cardiff - Crewe / Liverpool / Manchester)
- Wales & Wessex   (Cardiff / Bristol - Weymouth)
- North Wales Coast   (Birmingham / Crewe - Bangor / Holyhead / Llandudno)

Also, as we shall see later on, from 2010, DRS Class 37/4s would find passenger work on 'short set' passenger duties, vice DMU:

- Cumbrian Coast   (Carlisle - Barrow in Furness / Lancaster / Preston)
- Wherry Lines   (Norwich - Great Yarmouth / Lowestoft)

Sub-Classes

In the 1980s, the 37s were extensively refurbished (for extra longevity) and new sub-classes were introduced, except 37/3s which only received new bogies. The sub-classes became:

37/0	Unmodified
37/3	Re-bogied, but not refurbished
37/4	Refurbished, rewired, English Electric (EE) generator replaced with Brush alternator, ETH fitted
37/5	Refurbished, rewired, EE generator replaced with Brush Traction alternator
37/6	Ex-Class 37/5; further modified with through ETH wiring and RCH jumper cables
37/7	Refurbished, rewired, EE generator replaced with either a GEC G564AZ or Brush alternator, extra weight added to work heavier freight trains
37/9	Refurbished, rewired, EE generator replaced with Brush alternator, new engines: Mirrlees MB275Tt or Ruston RK270Tt

Operators

From the 1980s onwards, once locos had been refurbished they were operated by either EWS (English, Welsh & Scottish Railway) and DRS (Direct Rail Services), the latter using them on nuclear flask traffic emanating from Sellafield. However, a combination of their longevity and versatility attracted other operators to purchase second-hand examples from EWS (later DB Schenker) to work on spot-hire contract work, such as Colas Rail, Rail Operations Group and Loco Leasing Company. WCR (West Coast Railways) must also be included, as they have a mainline operators licence for work in the charter train and spot-hire market.

How many more years will we see Class 37s working on the main line?

(above) : *English, Welsh and Scottish Railway (EWS) colours of maroon and gold came on the scene in March 1996, when British Rail's trainload freight operations (Loadhaul, Mainline and Transrail) were sold to US-based Wisconsin Central, united under the EWS banner. Class 37 No.37057 was the first loco to be re-liveried, followed shortly after by No.37114 'City of Worcester. As No.37896 waits to leave the depot (bound for Fawley), No.37114 makes its way out of Eastleigh with a rake of 2-axle open wagons going to Westbury Yard.* (08/97)

**Assorted
Liveries**

EWS (above) : *EWS house colours of maroon & gold would soon become ubiquitous on their fleet of locos, just like in the BR Blue livery era. In this view, No.37503 (once fitted with split headcode indicator boxes) is passing Lea Marston on the Birmingham - Derby main line with 6G36, Bescot - Birch Coppice 'Enterprise'.* (09/03)

(top left) : *I know, it's a dull day, but I always enjoyed a visit to Healey Mills and couldn't resist this shot of No.37174 + Class 56 No.56107 double-heading 6E70, the 12:01 Castleton CE Depot - Doncaster departmental service, where the principle payload is welded rails.* (03/08)

(bottom left) : *Class 37/7 No.37706 slowly manoeuvres its way out of Briton Ferry yard to join the main line with 6E21, the 08:20 Baglan Bay - Humber empty pressurised polypropylene bogie tanks.* (08/98)

(below) : *Here, is No.37706 again, this time descending the 1 in 100 incline from Pilning to Severn Tunnel with a special (6G79) Westbury Yard - Newport ADJ departmental service, formed of Jarvis JFA 'Slinger' wagons.* 07/03)

Loadhaul (above) : *Perhaps, the most popular livery among enthusiasts, certainly striking. Loadhaul came on line in October 1994, along with two other regional freight companies (Mainline and Transrail), sporting black & orange colour. No.37713 enters Barnetby with 6D68, Lindsey - Leeds bitumen and fuel oil tanks.*   *(08/95)*

Railfreight Two-Tone Grey (below) : *Not a very inspiring livery, but the sub-sector 'decals' help to brighten the appearance. Class 37/8 No.37884 'Gartcosh' approaches Milford Junction with 6E39, the 06:45 Warrington Arpley - Hull Saltend empty 2-axle acid tanks. The loco sports Petrochemicals decals of blue & yellow waves with cast metal double arrows under the cab window at one end and a cast metal star and scroll emblem on the other end, which denotes it's allocation to Immingham TMD.*   *(07/95)*

Mainline (above) : *I particularly like this livery; Aircraft blue with silver stripe and Mainline branding. Here, passing Heamies Farm on the WCML, just north of Norton Bridge, is Class 37/7 No.37798, which is heading south with an unidentified departmental working, probably running to Bescot. The train is formed of empty YEA continuous welded rail wagons which have an operator's 'module' fitted at each end.*   *(05/00)*

(below) : *"Two For The Price of One" and the only time I have photographed a Class 37 / Class 60 combination. No.37074 + No.60047 double-head 6G85, Workington - Bescot, formed of some engineer's wagons and British Fuel 'tubs'. The train is passing Winwick, north of Warrington, on the WCML.*   *(04/97)*

EPS (above) : *European Passenger Services (now Eurostar) had 12 Class 37/6s (all modified Class 37/5s) to haul overnight international trains ('Nightstar') over the non-electrified sections of their routes in Britain. This never took place and 12 of them were transferred to DRS, who initially hired some to Freightliner. Here, Nos.37612 + 37610, now with DRS logo, pass through Eastleigh with 4O25, the 13:28 Ripple Lane - Southampton 'liner. (08/97)*

BR Blue, Large Logo (below) : *A throwback to the late '80s, when the Class 37/4s first appeared in BR blue with large logo. Here, 30 years later, DRS No.37402 'Stephen Middlemore' stands at Preston waiting to work 2C47, the 10:04 Preston - Barrow in Furness. Note the West Highland Terrier logo on the bodyside.   (07/16)*

Network Rail (above) : *Four Class 37s were converted to become Class 97/3s, refurbished for use on the Cambrian Lines which are signalled by ERTMS. They have also been used on Network Rail test trains, such as when No.97304 'John Tiley' (ex-No.37217) was seen at Bristol Temple Meads waiting to return to Derby RTC. The Network Rail livery is a rather uninspiring yellow.* (05/15)

Colas (below) : *The Colas Rail colours of orange, yellow and black are very reminiscent of Loadhaul and are also very pleasing on the eye. In this view, the OHLE test vehicle 'Mentor' is visiting Swindon, seen in the consist of 1Q18, Burton - Landore, hauled by 'split-box' Class 37 No.37099* (09/18)

(Selective Images)

Transrail (above) : *Following the introduction of EWS in to the railfreight market and with its new Class 66/0 locos, scenes like this one became increasingly rare, with many classes of heritage traction consigned to history. Class 37/8 No.37896 in Transrail livery, with a capital 'T' emblazoned on a blue circle, approaches Millbrook, Southampton, with 6V62 empty petroleum tanks for Holybourne and fuel oil for Eastleigh MPD, plus fuel oil for Western region diesel depots in the South West of England. The train runs via Eastleigh to detach the Holybourne and Eastleigh tanks. In the background are the giant cranes at Southampton container terminal.*   (08/97)

Railfreight Grey - Large Logo (top left) : *Class 37/5, No.37501 is seen in the centre road at Cardiff Central coupled up to Class 56 No.56036, also in Railfreight grey livery, waiting to go on to Canton TMD. No.56036 would later receive a repaint in Civil Engineer's yellow & grey livery.*   (09/86)

"Dutch" - Departmental Grey & Yellow (bottom left) : *This may not be the most aesthetically pleasing of liveries on the eye, grey with yellow band at the top of the bodyside, denoting allocation to the civil engineer's pool. Passing through Orton Mere cutting, Greenholme, split-box Class 37/0 No.37095 descends from Shap with 6G85, the 10:47 Workington - Bescot departmental, formed of a rake of empty continuous rail carriers.*   (04/97)

(Overleaf)

BR Blue (Page 14) : *Class 37/3 No.37308 is seen passing through Moreton cutting, near Didcot, with 6V38, the 09:02 Marchwood - Didcot Yard MoD stores, running late, but not before the shadows had spread across all the running lines. The loco was stored in 2000 and reverted to its 37308 identity, becoming part of the EWS heritage fleet, during which time it visited a number of heritage railways, while remaining in capital service.*   (11/02)

DRS Blue (Page 15) : *Nos.37069 + 37059 double head 4L46, Ditton - Purfleet intermodal and are seen passing through Tamworth Low level station on the WCML. The train is booked for a DRS Class 66/4 loco, but the 'tractors' are deputising on this occasion. DRS went on to introduce their famous 'Compass' livery for their entire loco fleet of Class 20s, 37s, 47s, 57s and 66s, plus the new Class 68s and 88s in later years.*   (05/06)

No.	Pool	Location	Working
Class 37s		**Fleet Survey**	**1st April 2020**
COLAS			
37025	COTS	Cardiff Canton	
37057	COTS	Ferme Park	1Q97, Ferme Park - Cambridge
37099	COTS	Melton Mowbray	1Z90, Melton Mowbray - Derby RTC
37116	COTS	Nottingham CMD	
37175	COTS	Nottingham CMD	
37219	COTS	Melton Mowbray	1Z90, Melton Mowbray - Derby RTC
37254	COTS	Derby RTC	0Z37, Derby RTC - Crewe CSFL
37418	COTS	Landore, Swansea	
37421	COTS	Nottingham SD	0Z37, Nottingham - Landore TMD
37607	COTS	Barrow HCR	
37610	COTS	Mossend	3Q40, Mossend - Inverness
37612	COTS	Cardiff Canton	3Q23, Cardiff Canton - Cardiff Canton
DRS			
37038	XHNC	Derby RTC	
37059	XHNC	Crewe, Gresty Bridge	
37069	XHNC	Eastleigh, Arlington	
37218	XHNC	Crewe, Gresty Bridge	
37259	XHNC	Carlisle Kingmoor	
37401	XHAC	Crewe Gresty Bridge	
37402	XHAC	Norwich Crown Point	5Z37, Norwich - Rotherham Masborough
37403	XHAC	Carlisle Kingmoor	
37405	XHAC	Carlisle Kingmoor	
37407	XHAC	Crewe Gresty Bridge	
37409	XHAC	Carlisle Kingmoor	
37419	XHAC	Carlisle Kingmoor	
37422	XHSS	Crewe, Gresty Bridge	
37423	XHAC	Crewe, Gresty Bridge	
37424	XHAC	Crewe, Gresty Bridge	
37425	XHAC	Derby RTC	
37602	XHHP	Eastleigh, Arlington	
37603	XHHP	Longtown	
37604	XHHP	Longtown	
37605	XHHP	Doncaster Roberts Road	
37606	XHHP	Crewe, Gresty Bridge	
37609	XHHP	Longtown	
37703	XHHP	Dollands Moor Cripple Siding	
37716	XHNC	Norwich Crown Point	5Z37, Norwich - Dereham
UK RAIL LEASING			
37905	UKRM	Leicester SD	
37906	UKRM	Leicester SD	
RAIL OPERATIONS GROUP			
37510	GROG	Leicester SD	
37601	GROG	Leicester SD	
37608	GROG	Norwich Crown Point	
37611	GROG	Norwich JS	
37800	GROG	Leicester SD	
37884	GROG	Leicester SD	

(right) : *Many ex-British Rail / EWS locos became available for sale to private individuals / operators, in this case Riley & Son, for the 'spot' hire market. Adorned in two-tone green livery, No.37197 passes through Horbury Cutting with Class 20s No.20096 + No.20168 en-route to the Keighley & Worth Valley Railway. No.37197 was transferred to Direct Rail Services in June 2006, withdrawn in 2012.* (08/03)

Setting the Scene

Towards the end of 2015, there were still pockets of semaphore signalling around the network, many in areas of, perhaps, secondary importance but, not all, as in and around Barnetby, which is on an extremely busy freight route.

The Port of Immingham is the busiest part of the London North Eastern Route of Network Rail in terms of freight, handling more than 260 daily rail freight movements. Immingham is the UK's largest port by tonnage and handles up to 55 million tonnes a year. It can handle up to 10 million tonnes of coal a year and can handle oil / bulk carrier cargoes up to 130,000 tonnes. The port also handles large volumes of biomass, animal feed, salt and grain and has two in-dock container terminals, which sees around 15 container vessel calls per week.

There are four specialist liquid-bulk terminals, incorporating 18 berths and around 25 percent of the country's oil-refinery capacity is located adjacent to the port at Humber and Lindsey refineries.

With demand for rail freight set to increase, it was decided that a complete resignalling of the area was needed so the infrastructure could handle this traffic more efficiently

The Closure

Over the Christmas of 2015 and 2016 New Year holiday season, a 17-day blockade ensued through Barnetby to enable the replacement of the mechanical signalling between Immingham, Scunthorpe and Cleethorpes with new colour light signalling. This re-signalling resulted in the decommissioning of 11 signal boxes, two gate boxes and 16 road crossings changed to remote operation, all of which controlled by York Rail Operating Centre.

The famous signal boxes at Wrawby Junction and Barnetby East remained in situ, albeit with no levers to pull heralding the passing of trains. The semaphores have succumbed to modern technology and progress. New colour signals were installed in time to mark the railway's re-opening and East Midlands Trains' 2T18, the 05:49 Cleethorpes - Newark North Gate became the first train to pass through Barnetby on 11th January 2016.

Before & After

I wanted to see the scene for myself, before the famous semaphore signals came down (2015) and after (2016); here are a few images I recorded for posterity.

Wrawby Junction signal box (above) : *This important signal box, now Grade II listed, used to control the confluence of routes from Lincoln, Retford and Scunthorpe towards Immingham and Cleethorpes. The large signal box of part-brick, part-wood, construction is a Great Central Railway Company type 5 design which opened in May 1916, fitted with a 137 lever Great Central Railway Company frame. The signal box was built and the lever frame manufactured by signalling contractor McKenzie & Holland Limited.*

BARNETBY (above**) :** *Looking back towards Wrawby Junction, five posts stand tall housing new colour light signals, as FHH Class 66/6 No.66617 approaches with 6K22, the 09:42 Santon - Immingham empty iron ore tipplers, The ever-lengtening shadow doing its best to spoil the shot. Meanwhile ......*

(below) : .... 12-months earlier, it's a different scene altogether and three, 3-way, junction bracket signals, control the lines to Lincoln (left), Brigg (centre) and Scunthorpe (right) at Wrawby Junction. The back end of a biomass service can be seen tailing off on the Scunthorpe road as Class 60 No.60010 approaches with another 6K22.

(above) : *A telephoto lens foreshortens this view of the semaphore signal, which guards the immediate passage of eastbound trains through Barnetby station. The road has been set for Class 153 - Single Car Super Sprinter - No.153 311 to enter for the Barnetby stop with 2T12, the 07:42 Newark North Gate - Grimsby Town..*

(below) : *There are a number of holding sidings on the 'Down' side of the running lines at Barnetby, which are used to stable trainsets awaiting the call to proceed to Immingham for their next turn of duty. A FHH Class 66/5 loco, No.66535, awaits the call with a rake of HXA bogie coal hoppers.*

A Selection of 'Arms'

"All Change" .... **Barnetby East** : (above) : Only the signal box remains in situ, all the semaphore signals have gone, although there is still a good vista of westbound freight, viewed from the station footbridge. FHH Class 66/6 No.66610 approaches with 6C75, the 10:33 Immingham - Scunthorpe steelworks loaded coal.

(below) : Ah, a view that had it all .... DBS Class 60 No.60015 hauls a rake of loaded TEA petroleum tanks past the signal box with 6M00, the 14:30 Humber - Kingsbury.

"The Footbridge"

I could not finalise this section without making reference to the infamous footbridge at Barnetby station which gives passengers access to all platforms. In the era of health & safety, disabled access, et al, around circa.1990, the old footbridge was demolished in favour of a new structure which, apparently, can be seen from outer space, just like the Great Wall of China.

If you were rushing to catch a train form the far island platform (Platforms 3 and 4), laden with suitcases, there is every chance you might miss your train, by the time you clambered up and over all the ramps and walkways, luggage and all - not sure how wheelchairs users are supposed to cope. When the station was manned, wheelchair users would have been assisted across the lines.

(above) : Loadhaul *No.56039 'Port of Hull' passes under the old footbridge with 6D86, the 12:50 Roxby - Grimsby empty Tioxide containers, which was situated further west along the platforms than the new structure.*

(top left) : *The new footbridge, which is set back further east, can be seen as FHH No.66617 runs through the station with 6T26, the 15:04 Immingham - Santon loaded iron ore tipplers.*

(bottom left) : *The new order of COVHOP wagons for a new fuel - Biomass - are branded 'Powering Tomorrow' and DB 'shed' No.66053 is seen working 6H77, the 16:30 Immingham - Drax loaded biomass.*

(below) : *Colas Rail Class 60 No.60076 'Dunbar' is in charge of 6E32, the 08:55 Preston Docks - Lindsey empty bitumen bogie tanks. The extended walkways for wheelchair users can clearly be seen.*

How This Came About

Barnetby is out on a limb, geographically speaking, and also a long way from Swindon, taking some four hours to get there by car. Bearing this in mind, I decided that when my friend Graham and I went to Barnetby to record the change in signalling, we would maximise the visits by taking in two branches over which I had never travelled:

> Barton-on-Humber
>
> Brigg

The latter presented more of a challenge, as the only passenger services run on a Saturday, three trains in each direction between Cleethorpes and Sheffield.

BARTON-on-HUMBER

The station, which was once the terminus of a 3¼-mile branch line from New Holland, is the terminus of the Barton line from Cleethorpes, situated 22¾ miles west of the resort. Approach to the branch was by a triangular junction at New Holland which enabled passenger trains to operate a New Holland Pier to Barton service in connection with the ferries and rail services from Cleethorpes. When the Humber Bridge opened the junction was removed and passenger services operated directly from Cleethorpes via the new platform at New Holland.

The original station was opened as part of the branch line from New Holland to Barton-on-Humber in 1849 and it was planned for the the railway to extend westwards to Winterton and beyond, though this never happened.

Cleethorpes

(left) : *Waiting patiently at Platform 2, Class 153 Single Car Super Sprinter No.153 324 will shortly whisk me away to Barton-on-Humber, running as 2F89 the 12:55hrs departure.*

I must say that I found the last leg of the line from New Holland to Barton-on-Humber disappointing, as I was expecting good views of the River Humber and the Humber suspension bridge, which did not materialise.

Barton-on-Humber

(left) : *This is the end of the line and terminus of the single line track to Barton-on-Humber. This end station, as is the case on many other branch lines, comprises a simple platform and nothing much else.*

Class 143 No.153 324 will now return with the 13:50hrs service back to Cleethorpes.

Timeline

Class 153 Single Car Super Sprinter

No.153 324

2F89, the 12:55 Cleethorpes - Barton on Humber

CLEETHORPES	**12:55 Dep.**
New Clee	Station request stop
Grimsby Docks	
Grimsby Town	
Great Coates	
Healing	
Stalinborough	
Habrough	
Habrough Jct.	
Ulceby	
Thornton Abbey	
Goxhill	
Oxmarsh L.C.	Service exchanges token
New Holland	
Barrow Haven	
BARTON-on-HUMBER	**13:46 Arr.**

Required Track : Habrough Jct. - Barton on Humber

10 Miles 74 Chains

Cleethorpes

(top right) : *The clock tower at Cleethorpes railway station is a Grade II listed landmark, which has been restored thanks to a £410,000 restoration project.*

Network Rail worked with the Railway Heritage Trust, TransPennine Express and Colt to dismantle the deteriorated timber clock tower and also refurbish it.

The clock mechanism and faces have also been restored.

(middle) : *What a pleasing sight, volunteer litter-pickers scour the beach at Cleethorpes to collect detritus swept in from the Humber estuary and that left by beachgoers.*

(right) : *Looking out across the estuary towards the north bank of the River Humber, MV.'Levana' heads towards a discharge jetty at either Hull Docks or the Port of Immingham*

The ship is an oil/chemical tanker, sailing under a Gibraltar flag, built in 2009 and is 8,816 gross tonnage.

The BRIGG Line

The railway station at Brigg in North Lincolnshire was built by the Great Grimsby and Sheffield Junction Railway (GG&SJR), opening in November 1848, before becoming part of the Manchester, Sheffield & Lincolnshire Railway main line between Grimsby and Manchester Piccadilly. The line was constructed in sections:

1st.   Ulceby to Brigg, opening in November 1848

2nd.   Brigg to Gainsborough, April 1849.

3rd.   The final link, from Woodhouse Junction (on the Sheffield - Beighton Junction section) to Gainsborough, opening in July 1849.

Brigg station opened on 16th July 1849, but is now unstaffed and managed by Northern Trains, who also operate all passenger trains serving it. The only buildings are a 'bus-style' shelter on each platform.

The station is served by three passenger trains in each direction on Saturdays only between Sheffield and Cleethorpes. Usage figures show that less than five passengers (setting up and down) travel on each train and there have been no timetabled weekday services at the station since October 1993, when they were withdrawn by British Rail.

On weekdays the line is used by freight traffic going to/from Immingham and it is an important diversionary route when the main line via Scunthorpe is closed. Another interesting feature is that the line still retains manual semaphore signalling with 'boxes at Brigg, Kirton Lime Sidings, Northorpe and Gainsborough Central. Of particular note, at the former Kirton Lime Sidings, is the superb Manchester, Sheffield & Lincolnshire Railway box, built in 1886. It is now Grade II listed and is an impressively tall structure, built hard against the road overbridge that spans the cutting at this location.

Cleethorpes (above) : *End of the line for Trans Pennine Express Class 185 DMU No.185 151, which brought me to Cleethorpes, having formed 1B68, the 087:53 ex-Manchester Airport. Alongside, Class 142 'Pacer' No.142 093 (above) is bringing up the rear of 2H00, which will be my ride to Sheffield via Brigg. By the time this service arrived in Sheffield, it was completely full with not a spare seat to be had!*

(top right): The station departure board showing the train servcie to Sheffield, via Brigg.

Brigg (bottom left) : *By the time the train arrived at Brigg, it was pouring with rain and I just had time to photograph the station sign, while the vehicle doors were open.*

Gainsborough Central (bottom right) : *A lone passenger has alighted at Gainsborough Central and proceeds towards the exit. Note the signal box, which opened as Gainsborough West in 1885 fitted with a 26 lever Manchester Sheffield & Lincolnshire Railway lever frame. It was renamed Gainsborough following the closure of Gainsborough East signal box and was further renamed Gainsborough Central.*

Timeline

Single Car Super Sprinter + Class 142 'Pacer'
2H00, the 11:00 Cleethorpes - Sheffield

CLEETHORPES	**11:14 Dep.**

New Clee
Grimsby Docks
Grimsby Town
Great Coates
Healing
Stalinborough
Habrough
Barnetby
Wrawby Jct.
Brigg
Kirton Lindsey
Gainsborough Central
Gainsborough Trent Jcts.
Retford
Worksop
Shireoaks
Kiveton Park
Kiveton Bridge
Woodhouse
Darnall
Woodburn Jct.
Nunnery Main Line Jct.

SHEFFIELD	**13:20 Arr.**

Required Track :

Wrawby Jct. - Gainsborough Trent East Jct.

20 Miles 68 Chains

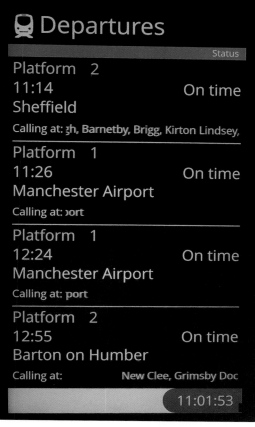

🚆 Departures

    Status

Platform   2
11:14   On time
Sheffield
Calling at: ʒh, Barnetby, Brigg, Kirton Lindsey,

Platform   1
11:26   On time
Manchester Airport
Calling at: ɔort

Platform   1
12:24   On time
Manchester Airport
Calling at: **port**

Platform   2
12:55   On time
Barton on Humber
Calling at: New Clee, Grimsby Doc

11:01:53

Background

Since 1979, I had travelled extensively across both passenger and freight lines in the UK, through a combination of early spotting trips by rail, '40' bashing and being an organiser of charter trains, which took in a huge swathe of the rail network.

I used my "Rail Atlas of Great Britain" as a guide and coloured a new line as and when I first travelled over it; there was, however, still a lot of track left to cover.

So, having previously enjoyed my branch line sojourns to Barton-on-Humber and Brigg during my trips to Barnetby, I decided to try and travel on the lines and branches that were still outstanding. The main branches were in England, Scotland and Wales:

South Wales	Maesteg / Merthyr Tydfil / Rhymney / Coryton / Cardiff Bay
South West	Severn Beach
London &	Kentish Town / Thameslink / Aylesbury / St Albans Abbey / Cheshunt / Enfield Town
Home Counties	Chingford / Hertford East / Southend Victoria / Braintree / Sudbury
	Colchester Town / Clacton on Sea / Walton on the Naze / Stansted Airport
	Aylesbury / Bicester / Henley / Marlow / Windsor
Anglia	Felixstowe / Sheringham / Newmarket
Midlands	Corby Line / Robin Hood Line / Redditch
North East	Bishop Auckland / Halifax
North West	West Kirby / New Brighton / Liverpool - Southport / Liverpool - Hunts Cross
	Ormskirk / Kirkby
	Blackpool South / Colne / Glossop / Hadfield / Manchester Airport
Scotland	Largs / Neilston / East Kilbride / Milngavie / Balloch / Helensburgh Central
	Larkhall / Lanark / Glasgow Central Low Level / Alloa / Tweedbank / North Berwick

~~~~~~~~~~~~~~~~~~~~~~~~~~~~~~~~

Norfolk / Suffolk / Essex
7th to 10th August 2016

NSE .... No, these initials do not represent Network South East, which would be appropriate in some respects, but simply Norfolk, Suffolk and Essex, the first of the visits I planned from 2016 to colour in the rest of the lines in my Rail Atlas.

I had already chalked off Felixstowe on a recent holiday and decided to leave the Newmarket line along with the two spurs into Stansted Airport for a later date. So, I concentrated on:

> Sheringham
>
> Braintree / Sudbury / Colchester Town / Clacton on Sea / Walton on the Naze

I also wanted to take advantage of the DRS loco-hauled trains on the Norwich - Great Yarmouth / Lowestoft services using two 'short' sets of Mk2 vehicles. Whilst distances between points were not that great, this allowed several trips to be made, plus the added bonus of semaphore signalling.

The latter, even more important, as these lines were due to be upgraded to colour light signalling in the next few years, controlled by Colchester Traffic Centre. I also did not want to miss out on some Class 37 and Class 68 haulage before replacement DMUs came on stream.

Sunday, 7th August 2016			
43030	Swindon - London Paddington	1L32, 08:00	Cardiff Central - London Paddington
90012	London Liv. St - Norwich	1P24, 11:30	London Liv. St - Norwich
156 417	Norwich - Sheringham	2S14, 14:36	Norwich - Sheringham
	Whittingham Jct - Sheringham	**28 miles 33 chains**	
156 417	Sheringham - Norwich	2S15, 15:42	Sheringham - Norwich
	Note : Annotations in red ink signify new track.		

Day 1

The 'Bittern Line'

This branch line in Norfolk, links Norwich to Sheringham and is named after the bittern, a rare bird found in the reeds and wetlands of Norfolk. The line is 30 miles 22 chains in length.

The line opened initially in 1874 between Norwich and North Walsham by the East Norfolk Railway, extended to Cromer and Sheringham in 1877.

The line is not electrified and is double-track from Norwich to Hoveton and Wroxham, where it becomes single-track with a passing loop at North Walsham. A reversal at Cromer is needed to complete the remaining 3 miles and 36 chains to Sheringham.

The section between Sheringham and Holt (closed in the 1960s) is still in use as a heritage railway line, operated as the North Norfolk Railway (NNR). After 36 years, the link between the Bittern line and the North Norfolk Railway was reinstated in 2010 with the opening of a new level crossing at Sheringham.

The line was re-signalled in 2000, leading to the closure of a number of mechanical signal boxes, and control moved to Trowse Swing Bridge control room. There is no scheduled freight on the line except for a GBRf-operated flow of gas condensate from North Walsham to Harwich. Some OTP (On Track Plant) vehicles also travel onto the NNR for testing

Norwich

(above) : As I looked from the carriage window aboard my train from London, I could see two Class 68s stabled in Jubilee Carriage Sidings, Nos. 68019 and No.68016, each end of three Mk2s.

The smart looking livery of turquoise and white was introduced on 10th June 1998, infinitely better than the current Greater Anglia colour scheme of white with a black stripe!

To complement the existing Class 37 loco-hauled diagram, Abelio Greater Anglia introduced a second loco-hauled diagram from Norwich to Great Yarmouth / Lowestoft, in addition to the existing DRS Class 37s in use on a Monday - Saturday diagram, working in top 'n' tail formation. This change came into effect from Monday, 11th July 2016.

This second replacement was needed due to the continuing shortage of DMUs and the loss of Class 170 No.170 204, which was under long-term repair.

Opposite :

(top left) : Arrival at Norwich .... Class 90 No.90012 'Royal Anglian Regiment' sits at the end of Platform 2 having brought in 1P24 from London Liverpool Street. Two DRS Class 68s are also in view; No.68023 'Achilles' on the left (standby loco) and No.68016 'Fearless' on the far right.

Cromer

(above) : *Cromer is a small terminus and services running between Norwich and Sheringham have to reverse here in order to continue their journey. Originally two stations served the town, 'Cromer High Station' and 'Cromer Beach', the latter opened as Cromer Beach on 16th June 1887 and was renamed Cromer on 20th October 1969, following the closure of Cromer High station in 1954. It is 26 miles 52 chains from Norwich.*

This was my train, No.156 417, seen at Cromer, waiting to leave for Sheringham after a reversal.

(below) : *Cromer signal box is the former Midland & Great Northern Joint Railway signal box, which is no longer in use following its closure in 2000, but is a listed building. It is built of concrete blocks, the favourite building material of the line's engineer, William Marriott, although the front panels are faced with brick. The frame originally contained 29 levers controlling just the station area, but this was enlarged in 1954 to 35.*

Sheringham

(right) : *The BR station sign at Sheringham with the distinctive double arrows logo. Even after all this time since the demise of British Rail, this unique design is synonymous with railways and recognised by people the length and breadth of the land.*

Sheringham railway station is the northern terminus of the Bittern Line, serving the town of Sheringham. It is 30 miles 22 chains in the 'down' direction (ie. north west, geographically speaking) from Norwich.

The present station opened in January 1967 and replaced the original station, originally opened by the Midland and Great Northern Joint Railway, which is located on the other side of the level crossing. This original station subsequently became the terminus of the North Norfolk Railway.

(below) : *As you can see the weather was excellent, blue skies and unbroken sunshine and pleasingly hot.*

Days 2 and 3

The 'Wherry Lines'

These two days were spent working the diagrams between Norwich and Great Yarmouth / Lowestoft; one diagram worked by top 'n' tail Class 37s, the other top 'n' tail Class 68s. A selection of images follows to illustrate my journeys; the only trouble 'bashing' is that you cannot do two things at once, so there was, regrettably, no photographing at the lineside.

History

The Wherry Lines are branch lines in East Anglia, which link Norwich with Great Yarmouth (Norfolk) and Lowestoft (Suffolk), both of which are end of line terminuses. These lines pass through the Broads of Norfolk and Suffolk and the name 'Wherry' is taken from the Norfolk wherries, a boat used to transport goods and people around the Broads, before the advent of road and rail.

The route was opened in three stages:

1. 1844 : Norwich to Great Yarmouth by the Norwich and Yarmouth Railway, via Reedham.
2. 1847 : Reedham to Lowestoft, as part of the Norfolk Railway.
3. 1883 : Norwich to Great Yarmouth via Acle by the Great Eastern Railway, in two parts:
   March 1883 : Breydon Junction to Acle.
   June 1883 : Through to Brundall.

The line from Norwich to Lowestoft is double-track throughout, but the two Great Yarmouth branches that diverge from Brundall via Acle and from Reedham via Berney Arms are single-track. Of note, Berney Arms is one of the most remote and least-used stations on the rail network; miles from the nearest road and so accessible only by train, on foot, or by boat, the River Yare being close by.

Route Mileage

Norwich - Great Yarmouth

18 miles 29 chains (via Acle)   20 miles 45 chains (via Reedham)

Norwich - Lowestoft

23 miles 22 chains

(above) : *No.68023 'Fearless' sits in an old bay platform adjacent to Norwich Thorpe station, waiting to be called upon in the event of a failure materialising on either No.68016 or No.68019.*

During my visit, No.68023 was not called into action.

(right) : *My '3 Days in 7' Anglia Plus rover ticket, which would cover me in an area bounded by Sheringham, Great Yarmouth, Lowestoft and Ipswich.*

Norwich Departures

(above) : *The two loco hauled sets wait at Norwich for their respective departures:*

      No.37419 'Carl Haviland 1954-2012' on 2P18, the 10:36 Norwich - Great Yarmouth

      No.68019 'Brutus' on 2J70, the 10:05 Norwich - Lowestoft.

(below) : *A closer look at No.37419 sitting in Platform 4, atop three DRS liveried Mk2 vehicles, with the other Class 37/4 working the set, No.37422 on the rear.*

LOWESTOFT (above) : *Class 68 No.68019 'Brutus' has arrived at the Suffolk terminus with 2J70, the 10:05 Norwich - Lowestoft, sitting alongside Class 170 No.170 205 which has come in off the East Suffolk Line with 2D72, the 09:17 Ipswich - Lowestoft. On this day, I stayed with the 68s and made six trips in all.*

(below) : *The 'peg' is raised for the imminent departure of No.68016 'Fearless' on 2J73, the 10:57hrs departure for Norwich, a journey which will take about 45 minutes to complete. The DRS 'Compass' logo is prominent on the bodyside of No.68016, which carries a dark blue and aquamarine livery.*

GREAT YARMOUTH (above) : *The run from Norwich takes only 30 minutes and so I was able to complete several return trips between Norwich and Great Yarmouth during the day, plus a few to Lowestoft. Here, unbranded DRS Class 37/4 No.47422 waits to leave the Norfolk terminus with 2P13, the 09:17 Great Yarmouth - Norwich.*

(below) : *Due to an 'incident' at Acle, train 1P11 was cancelled and, in order to get the train set back in diagram, it left Great Yarmouth as ECS, running via Reedham. No.68019 'Brutus' brings up the rear of 5P11, the 08:46 Great Yarmouth - Norwich ECS with No.68016 'Fearless' leading.*

WHERRY
SIGNAL BOXES

Lowestoft (left) At the time of my visit, this was t*he most easterly signal box on the entire rail network.*

This Great Eastern Railway box dates back to 1885 with a 61-lever frame.

Prior to the introduction of colour light signalling, controlled by Colchester Signalling Centre, the 'box was open to the public on Saturday and Sunday, September 14-15 and 21-22 in 2019.

Acle (middle)

The signal box is a type GER 3/S&F, platform-fitted former Great Eastern 'box opening in 1883 and is fitted with a 20 lever frame.

Acle is the only station on this branch of the Wherry Line which has a passing loop.

Somerleyton (opposite)

All four surviving swing bridges across the Norfolk Broads are still in use.

One of these is at Somerleyton.

It is located a short distance to the north-west of Somerleyton railway station. The bridge takes the railway line over the River Waveney - 47ft wide and a clearance of 8.5ft.

The box itself is brick-built of Great Eastern design, dates from 1886 and has a lever frame of McKenzie & Holland origin, being of their later tappet type which had shorter levers.

Oulton Broad (left)

The signal box at Oulton Broad North dates from the doubling of the line onwards into Lowestoft in 1901. Alongside is a busy level crossing, on which the gates were replaced by lifting barriers in 1974.

The signal box has also controlled the junction with the East Suffolk line ever since Oulton Broad Junction box was decommissioned in 1929. Oulton Broad has a second signal box, Oulton Broad South, which is on the East Suffolk Line.

Through the Carriage Window - 'Wherry' Distractions

Stracey Arms (above) : *This is Stracey Arms mill, built in 1883 for Robert Barnes of Great Yarmouth, and is a typical sight in this part of the world. During WWII it was used as a pillbox, fitted with an anti-aircraft turret to protect against attacks against RAF bases within East Anglia.*

Cantley (below) : *I did notice that all the small stations were well kept and tidy, some with floral displays as in here at Cantley. The flower bed contains lavender, dahlias, gladioli and busy lizzies.*

Reedham Swing Bridge (above) : *Returning from Lowestoft, this was the view of Reedham Swing Bridge as my train curved round towards it, slowing to cross the River Yare. The original single track bridge was commissioned by Sir Samuel Morton Peto in the 1840s to allow the passage of wherry boats. The current bridge dates from 1902/1903 prior to the doubling of the track.*

Somerleyton (below) : *Leaving Somerleyton behind, looking out across the field, I could see how the railway climbs slightly to the swing bridge, built in 1905 to carry the double track Norwich - Lowestoft line over the River Waveney. Note the two semaphore signals, the nearest being constructed of concrete.*

Monday, 8th August 2016

68019	Norwich - Great Yarmouth	2P10, 08:09	Norwich - Great Yarmouth
68016	Great Yarmouth - Norwich	2P11, 08:46	Great Yarmouth - Norwich
68019	Norwich - Lowestoft	2J70, 10:05	Norwich - Lowestoft
68016	Lowestoft - Norwich	2J73, 10:57	Lowestoft - Norwich
68019	Norwich - Lowestoft	2J74, 12:05	Norwich - Lowestoft
68016	Lowestoft - Norwich	2J77, 12:57	Lowestoft - Norwich

Class 68s work in top 'n' tail mode

Fill In Moves

90005	Norwich - Ipswich	1P43, 14:00	Norwich - London Liverpool St
90015	Ipswich - Norwich	1P34, 14:00	London Liverpool St - Norwich
90014	Norwich - Ipswich	1P57, 17:30	Norwich - London Liverpool St
90004	Ipswich - Norwich	1P54, 18:10	London Liverpool St - Norwich

Tuesday, 9th August 2016

37419	Norwich - Great Yarmouth	2P12, 08:36	Norwich - Great Yarmouth
37422	Great Yarmouth - Norwich	2P13, 09:17	Great Yarmouth - Norwich
68019	Norwich - Lowestoft	2J70, 10:05	Norwich - Lowestoft
68016	Lowestoft - Norwich	2J73, 10:57	Lowestoft - Norwich
37419	Norwich - Great Yarmouth	2P20, 12:36	Norwich - Great Yarmouth
37422	Great Yarmouth - Norwich	2P21, 13:17	Great Yarmouth - Norwich

Class 68s work in top 'n' tail mode

Class 37s work in top 'n' tail mode

Fill In Moves

90012	Norwich - Ipswich	1P43, 14:00	Norwich - London Liverpool St
90034	Ipswich - Colchester	1P49, 15:30	London Liverpool St - Norwich

---

(Previously) :

Acle (page 44) : *This little station lies 10 miles and 34 chains east of Norwich on the northern of the two lines to Great Yarmouth and the site of the only passing loop.*

I had arrived there behind No.68016 'Fearless' on 2P11, the 08:46 Great Yarmouth - Norwich and had to wait for No.37419 'Carl Haviland 1954-2012' to come off the single line section with 2P12, the 08:36 Norwich - Great Yarmouth. This is the view from the station footbridge looking at No.37419 about to enter the station.

Reedham Swing Bridge (page 45) : *The benefit of travelling in Mk2 vehicles is that I could pull down the carriage door window and take photographs, like this example.*

No.68016 'Fearless' is seen bringing up the rear of 2J70, the 10:05 Norwich - Lowestoft as the train leaves the swing bridge behind.

Time to Leave

(above) : *This was my last run out of Lowestoft; No.68016 'Fearless' on 2J73, the 10:57 Lowestoft - Norwich. I had a very enjoyable and rewarding couple of days chasing 37s and 68s in and out of Norwich to Great Yarmouth and Lowestoft, knowing that only a few years later these locos and all the semaphore signalling would be gone from the Wherry Lines. I'm so glad I made the effort.*

(below) : *Arriving back in Norwich, it was time to venture south for the next leg of my journey; the branch lines of Essex, using Colchester as a base. I departed from Norwich behind Class 90 No.90012 'Royal Anglian Regiment' on 1P43, the 14:00hrs service to London Liverpool Street, which was quite fitting as this was the loco I arrived with at Norwich on the Sunday. I decided to break my journey in Ipswich.*

I managed to photograph DRS Class 90 No.90034 in Direct Rail Services dark blue livery, with a DB sticker on the front cab, before I boarded the train. The loco was on hire to Anglia Railways with the 'Pretendolino' Mk3 set, which is seen arriving at Ipswich with 1P49, the 15:30 Norwich - London Liverpool Street.

Day 4

Essex Branches

I had already confirmed my one night stay in a Premier Inn in Colchester for Tuesday evening, the hotel conveniently located in Cowdray Avenue, about 5 - 10 minutes walk, south of the railway station.

The itinerary for the day ahead had been planned a few weeks earlier and, if everything went to plan, I would leave Colchester on the 15:30hrs service to London Liverpool Street, hauled by one of the excellent Class 90s.

The friendly and helpful travel centre staff at Swindon railway station, advised me that the most economical way to travel on the selected branches, was to purchase single tickets, in advance, on a 'point to point' basis from one location to another, starting and finishing back at Colchester.

Ticketing Arrangements

1. Colchester - Clacton on Sea

2. Clacton on Sea - Colchester

3. Thorpe Le Soken
   - Walton on the Naze

4. Walton on the Naze
   - Thorpe Le Soken

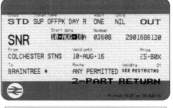

5. Colchester - Braintree

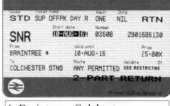

6. Braintree - Colchester

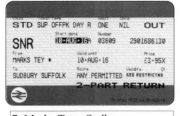

7. Marks Tey - Sudbury

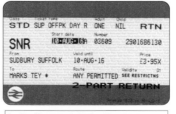

8. Sudbury - Marks Tey

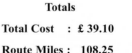

Totals	
Total Cost	: £ 39.10
Route Miles :	108.25

Starting Point - Colchester

Colchester railway station is on the Great Eastern Main Line (GEML), 51 miles and 52 chains out of London Liverpool Street situated between Marks Tey to the west and Manningtree to the east. Colchester is also the junction for the 'Sunshine Coast Line' to both Clacton-on-Sea and Walton-on-the-Naze, plus services to and from Colchester Town.

The junction referred to above is interesting, as it is grade-separated, meaning trains branching to and from Colchester Town or the Sunshine Coast Line do not cross the GEML.

Colchester station was opened in 1843 by the Eastern Counties Railway.

(above) : *This is the old station building at Colchester, which is now at the rear, the main ticket office is a modern glass-fronted design, sited on the north side of the station, access to the platforms is via a subway.*

Wednesday, 10th August 2016			
321 338	Colchester - Clacton on Sea	1N12,	08:16 London Liv. St - Clacton on Sea
	Colchester - Clacton on Sea		
321 331	Clacton on Sea - Thorpe Le Soken	1N33,	10:05 Clacton on Sea - London Liv. St
321 339	Thorpe Le Soken - Walton on the Naze	2F26,	09:56 Colchester - Walton on the Naze
	Thorpe Le Soken - Walton on the Naze		
321 339	Walton on the Naze - Colchester	2F35,	11:00 Walton on the Naze - Colchester
	Hythe Jct - Colchester Town - East Gate Jct - Colchester Jct		
360 107	Colchester - Witham	1Y39,	11;52 Ipswich - London Liv. St
321 322	Witham - Braintree	1F22,	11:48 London Liv. St - Braintree
	Witham - Braintree		
321 322	Braintree - Witham	1F43,	13:00 Braintree - London Liv. St
360 120	Witham - Marks Tey	2F48,	12:38 London Liv. St - Colchester Town
156 407	Marks Tey - Sudbury	2T18,	14:01 Marks Tey - Sudbury
	Marks Tey - Sudbury		
156 407	Sudbury - Marks Tey	2T19,	14:26 Sudbury - Marks Tey
360 102	Marks Tey - Colchester	1Y20,	14:02 London Liv. St - Ipswich
90007	Colchester - London Liv. St	1P53,	16:30 Norwich - London Liv. St
43021	London Paddington - Swindon	1G88,	19:48 London Paddington - Swindon

Note : Annotations in red ink signify new track.

COLCHESTER

(above) : *After its closure in the 1990s, Colchester depot is now used to stable DMUs/EMUs and is currently known as Colchester Carriage Servicing Depot. A DRS Class 37 can be seen stabled in a reception siding.*

Formerly coded 30E, the depot had a small allocation of Class 08 shunting locos, one of which was No.08767. This loco was the 13th on my list to finish seeing all locos/electric locos listed in my Ian Allan shedbook. I finally tracked it down, stabled at Harwich Town on 5th June 1976.

(below) : *At the time of my visit, inter-city services between London and Norwich were in the hands of Class 90s + Mk3s + DVT which, as I found, performed admirably. Class 90 No.90013 decelerates for the Colchester stop with 1P45, the 14:30 Norwich - London Liverpool Street.*

(above) : *Here it comes, my first train on Wednesday morning, to take me on the 'Sunshine Coast' Line to visit Clacton and Walton.*

Class 321 EMU No.321 338 pulls into the station with 1N12, the 08:16 London Liverpool Street - Clacton on Sea service.

This example, along with many other units I would see, carried the Greater Anglia livery of white with a black stripe, some decidedly tired and work-weary grey in appearance.

(right) : *Class 321 No.321 335 has pulled into Platform 5 with 2F65, the 16:00 Walton on the Naze - Colchester, where many passengers will await the arrival of the next fast train to London.*

That will be 1P51, the 16:00hrs ex-Norwich which is making its approach to the station headed by No.90007 'Sir John Betjeman'.

For the record, due to the unusual layout of platforms, Colchester station has the longest platform in the UK, as the entire length from platform 3 to 4 measures 2,034ft. Gloucester is the second longest at 1,977ft 4ins..

The 'Sunshine Coast' Line

Background

The term 'Sunshine Coast Line' is the marketing name of what was originally the 'Tendring Hundred' Railway Line, which was completed in stages:

1. A short section of line was built by the Colchester, Stour Valley, Sudbury & Halstead Railway to the port village of Hythe, opening for freight traffic in March 1847.

2. In 1859, the Tendring Hundred Railway Company was formed. The line extended to Wivenhoe, which opened in May 1863 for both passenger and goods services from Colchester. By this time, this extension of the line had been taken over by the Great Eastern Railway.

3. By May 1867, the route finally reached Walton on the Naze.

4. In March 1866, a new station in Colchester opened, called St. Botolph's.

   Renamed Colchester Town in July 1991 by British Rail.

5. The spur off the main line from Thorpe-le-Soken to Clacton, built by the Clacton-on-Sea Railway, opened 15 years after the Walton branch opened.

   Its name changed to Clacton-on-Sea in May 2007.

Section Mileage

Colchester *to* Clacton-on-Sea	18 miles	4 chains
Clacton-on-Sea *to* Thorpe-le-Soken	4 miles	49 chains
Thorpe-le-Soken *to* Walton-on-the-Naze	5 miles	8 chains
Walton-on-the-Naze *to* Colchester Town	17 miles	58 chains
Colchester Town *to* Colchester	2 miles	14 chains

Thorpe-le-Soken (above) : *The old signal box is situated on the island platform at the station and was closed in 2009 when the 'Sunshine Coast' Line was re-signalled, controlled by a new panel at Colchester power signal box.*

Clacton-on-Sea

(above) : *Class 321 EMU No.321 315 is seen running into the EMU Sidings and past Clacton-on-Sea signal box, a former Great Eastern type 7 structure dating from the 1891 station enlargement, which replaced an older structure. The box has a 69 lever frame.*

(below) : *For my return journey, I sat in the leading car, No.321 331, which I rode with as far as Thorpe Le Soken, where I would change trains for the run to Walton-on-the-Naze. The train is 1N33 to London.*

Through the Carriage Window

Frinton-on-Sea (above / opposite) : *As my train stopped at Frinton-on-Sea, I could not help but notice the beautiful murals painted on the walls of the station. However, looking through a carriage window pane is not easy, but I think the results are acceptable.*

The mural marks the 125th anniversary of the railway arriving at the Essex seaside town. The artist is David Nash and the mural showcases iconic images associated with this beautiful seaside resort, including colourful beach huts, the clock shelter and a steam loco once associated with the Great Eastern.

The steam loco depicted in the mural above is No.70000, a British Railways (BR) Standard Class 7 4-6-2 Pacific (also known as 'Britannia' class), which is now preserved. It was built at Crewe, completed in January 1951, and the first of 55 locos in the class. It was named 'Britannia' at London Marylebone Station on 30th January 1951.

'Britannia' was initially based at Stratford (30A) and regularly worked passenger expresses to Norwich and Great Yarmouth, particularly associated with the Hook Continental boat train to Harwich.

Walton-on-the-Naze (below) : *Arriving at Walton-on-the-Naze, I could see across the rooftops to the Port of Felixstowe, which is the UK's busiest container port, dealing with some 50% of Britain's containerised trade. Moored at the port are two large container ships from Yang Ming and Maersk shipping lines.*

"Restricted Space"

Walton-on-the-Naze (above) : *A problem often faced when arriving at many branch line termini, the difficulty of getting any reasonable photographic record, due to a lack of space. Here, is the first of two images on this page to illustrate this .... I could not go back any further and this is the result; No.321 339 on arrival at Walton-on-the-Naze having brought me the 5 miles and 8 chains along the single line from Thorpe-le-Soken.*

Colchester Town (left)

The end of the platform falls away immediately behind me and I'm nearly on top of the unit, in an attempt to photograph the train.

The train service is 2F35, the 11:00 Walton-on-the-Naze - Colchester.

Colchester Town is a single track terminus, served by a 13 chain section of single line track from Colne Junction.

To the east of the station, Colne Junction is the western extremity of a triangle which gives access towards Colchester station to the west and Hythe station to the east. The curve northwards from Colne Junction to East Gates Junction is tight, so there is a continuous check rail which necessitates slow passage.

It was now time to complete the 8-minute, 1 mile 42 chains, run into Colchester and do the last two branches; Braintree and Sudbury.

Witham (above) : *Thirteen miles south west of Colchester is Witham, where I changed trains for the 6 mile and 30 chains ride along the single line to Braintree. While waiting at Witham, I was fortunate to see an example (in fact, a pair!) of my favourite electric locos; Freightliner's Class 86/6, now 50 years young.*
Nos. 86627 + 86228 approach with a fully laden 4M67, the 11:13 Felixstowe North - Trafford Park freightliner.

Braintree (below) : *I reached Braintree aboard another Class 321 EMU, this time No.321 322 on 1F22, the 11:48 London Liverpool Street - Braintree and I would return to Witham on the 1F43 service back to London. In this view, No.321 322 waits departure time and marks the last electrified branch line I would visit in Essex.*

Marks Tey (above) : *2-car 'Super Sprinter' No.156 407 stands at Platform 3 waiting to depart with 2T18, the 14:01 Marks Tey - Sudbury, an 11 mile 67 chains journey, which takes 20 minutes to complete.*

Marks Tey (above) : *Marks Tey is only five miles south west of Colchester and the junction for the Sudbury branch. While waiting for my train, I was able to photograph 'Powerhaul' Class 70 No.70017 heading south with 4M93, the 13;34 Felixstowe - Lawley Street freightliner. The newly laid track in the foreground leads to the branch.*

Sudbury (below) : *End of the line, but once the Stour Valley Railway that ran between Shelford, near Cambridge, and Marks Tey, opening in sections between 1849 and 1865. The route from Shelford to Sudbury closed in March 1967, leaving only the Sudbury - Marks Tey section, known as the Gainsborough Line. Standing alongside a shelter decorated with a floral mural, No.156 407 is ready to leave and take me back to Marks Tey.*

Through the Carriage Window - London Landmarks

As Class 90 No.90007 'Sir John Betjeman' hurtled towards London with 1P53, the 16:30 Norwich - London Liverpool Street, within the final few miles out, the fantastic London skyline of modern architecture was a joy to behold.

Many of the landmarks I could easily identify, but others were new to me. The two images opposite give you an idea. However, in the top image, almost lost in a cornucopia of modern design is Christ Church, Spitalfields, dwarfed by the Salesforce Tower; an Anglican church built between 1714 - 1729 on Commercial Street in London Borough of Tower Hamlets, on its western border facing the City of London,

(Opposite) :

(top - from left to right) :**20 Fenchurch Street**, *nicknamed the 'Walkie-Talkie' because of its distinctive shape. Completed in 2014, it is 4] 551ft tall.*

30 St Mary Axe, *informally known as the 'Gherkin'. It opened 2004, has 41 floors and is 591 ft tall, standing on the former sites of the Baltic Exchange and Chamber of Shipping,*

122 Leadenhall Building *is primarily an office building, standing 738ft tall. It is famous for its wedge shape. Inclined at ten degrees vertically, the building is referred to as the 'Cheesegrater' thanks to its form.*

110 Bishopsgate *is the Salesforce Tower (formerly, the Heron Tower) 755 ft tall and its 92 ft mast makes it the tallest building in the City of London financial district and the third tallest in Greater London and the United Kingdom, after the Shard in Southwark and One Canada Square at Canary Wharf.*

(bottom) : *The view on the other side of the line is not so spectacular, save for the two architectural masterpieces which were designed and constructed for the 2012 London Olympic Games, which are from left to right:*

Olympic Stadium, *now known as the 'London Stadium'. It opened on 6th May 2012, constructed to host the 2012 Olympic and Paralympic Games, renovated between 2013 - 2016 and is the present home of West Ham United football club.*

ArcelorMittal Orbit, *often referred to as the 'Orbit Tower' or simply 'Orbit' is a 376ft high sculpture and observation tower in the Queen Elizabeth Olympic Park in Stratford. It is Britain's largest piece of public art and a permanent lasting legacy of London's hosting of the 2012 Summer Olympic and Paralympic Games.*

"End of the Line" .... London Liverpool Street

(above) : *Class 90 No.90007 'Sir John Betjeman' sits on the blocks after safely bringing me aboard train 1P53 back to London from Colchester. Sitting alongside is No.90005 'Vice-Admiral Lord Nelson' which arrived with 9P63 from Norwich - all in all, an excellent trip!*

Setting The Scene

According to my records, I had only once travelled on the Merseyrail system and that was only briefly, on 23rd July 1982 during a week-long North West rail rover.

I arrived at Liverpool Lime Street late evening behind Class 40 No.40180, which had worked the 21:43hrs service from Preston; a 'portion' off 1M40, Glasgow Central - Manchester Victoria. The plan was to get to Chester and join 1D77, the 22:40 Manchester Victoria - Holyhead, which connected at Holyhead with a sailing to Ireland.

At Lime Street, along with my friend Michael, we swiftly made our way to the lower level and catch a service to Chester, by way of under the River Mersey, serving the principal stations of:

Birkenhead / Rock Ferry / Bebington / Port Sunlight / Spital / Bromborough / Hooton

This train service was formed of Class 503 EMUs, first introduced in 1938, but had all been withdrawn by 1985. Our train duly arrived on time, as did Class 40 No.40055 with 1D77 bound for Holyhead.

Consequently, the rest of the 3rd Rail system remained untravelled, until now ....

Background

The large Merseyrail network was formed in 1977 by merging separate rail lines by constructing new tunnels under Liverpool city centre and Birkenhead. It serves Liverpool and the surrounding Liverpool City Region, a part of Serco-Abellio.

The network is composed of two lines known as the '**Northern Line**' and the '**Wirral Line**' which are electrified throughout using the third-rail 750 V DC system, supplied and controlled by the Electric Control Room at Sandhills. The Merseyrail third rail network has 68 stations and 75 miles of route, of which 6.5 miles are underground.

Network Map

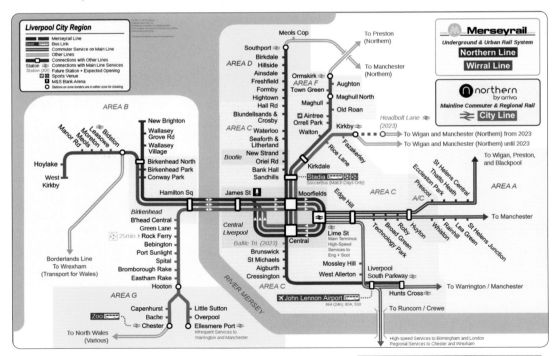

(Courtesy Kvj : Commons.wikipedia)

The Routes

There are two principal routes:

1) Northern Line

Hunts Cross to Southport

Liverpool Central to Ormskirk

Liverpool Central to Kirkby

2) Wirral Line

Liverpool Lime Street to New brighton

Liverpool Lime Street to West Kirby

Liverpool Lime Street to Chester

Liverpool Lime Street to Ellesmere Port

July 2017

During a time spent in the North West (4th - 7th July 2017), I allocated one day to complete the Merseyrail system, as per my Rail Atlas, which I nearly achieved. However, for some inexplicable reason, I overlooked the section to Hunts Cross, so I would have to come back and do this line in September the same year, when I covered some other lines in the North West.

Thursday, 6th July 2017

142 003	Preston - Ormskirk Preston - Ormskirk	2F04, 08:43 Preston - Ormskirk
508 120	Ormskirk - Sandhills Ormskirk - Sandhills	2G31, 09:20 Ormskirk - Liverpool Central
508 127	Sandhills - Southport Sandhills - Southport	2S15, 09:36 Hunts Cross - Southport
508 127	Southport - Liverpool Central Sandhills - Liverpool Central	2U22, 10:58 Southport - Hunts Cross
508 130	Liverpool Central - West Kirby Liverpool Central - West Kirby	2W20, 11:21 West Kirby - West Kirby
508 130	West Kirby - Birkenhead North	2W25, 12:36 West Kirby - West Kirby
507 005	Birkenhead North - New Brighton Birkenhead North - New Brighton	2N25, 12:23 New Brighton - New Brighton
507 005	New Brighton - Liverpool Central	2N29, 13:23 New Brighton - New brighton
508 139	Liverpool Central - Kirkby Walton Junction - Kirby	2K30, 14:05 Liverpool Central - Kirkby

Fill In Moves

150 134	Kirkby - Manchester Victoria Kirkby - Wigan Wallgate Crows Nest Jct - Salford Crescent	2J66, 14:44 Kirkby - Blackburn
150 110	Manchester Victoria - Wigan Wallgate Lostock Jct - Crows Nest Jct	2F81, 15:15 Huddersfield - Wigan Wallgate

September, 22nd September 2017

507 005	Sandhills - Hunts Cross Liverpool Central - Hunts Cross	2U21, 10:43 Southport - Hunts Cross

Note : Annotations in red ink signify new track.

Merseyrail Diary

(1)   Preston - Ormskirk   **142 003**

Faringdon Curve Jct - Ormskirk   **13 miles 59 chains**

PRESTON (above) : My starting point .... *Class 142 'Pacer' unit No.142 003 sits in a bay platform (3a) at the south end of Preston station, which will form 2F04, the 08:43 Preston - Ormskirk*

Ormskirk

The railway station in Ormskirk is a cross-platform interchange between Merseyrail services from Liverpool Central and Northern Trains services from Preston. The station building is Grade II listed.

The station was built by the East Lancashire Railway, linking Liverpool - Ormskirk - Preston, opening in April 1849. From May 1859, the station was owned by the Lancashire and Yorkshire Railway, followed by the London, Midland and Scottish Railway in 1923, before being nationalised in January 1948, when it became part of the London Midland Region.

The line from Liverpool was subsequently electrified in 1913.

Following the restructuring of the rail network post-Beeching, there were two main through platforms. The electric Liverpool commuter trains would pull into the southern bay platform, a practice which ended following the withdrawal of through trains between Liverpool and Preston via this route. From October 1969, local services from Preston towards Liverpool were either withdrawn or terminated at Ormskirk

Effective May 1970, the line was split with all trains using the former Liverpool platform.

(opposite) : *Two views following my arrival at Ormskirk station, where you can see that it was only a short walk down the platform to board my first 'Merseyrail' service of the day; No.508 120 on 2G31, the 09:20hrs to Liverpool Central, which I would take as far as Sandhills for the next leg to Southport.*

(2)   Ormskirk - Sandhills   **142 003**   **10 miles 60 chains**

ORMSKIRK

SOUTHPORT

(above) : *A panoramic view of the six platforms in use at Southport.*

(below) : *Class 508 EMU No.508 127 has arrived at Southport with 2S15 from Hunts Cross and passengers now make their way towards the exit. No.508 103 stands alongside. As you can see, the impressive trainshed glass canopy lets in 'shedloads' of light on to the platforms.*

Merseyrail Diary

(3)	Sandhills - Southport	508 127	16 miles 60 chains

SOUTHPORT

The station is the terminus of the Southport branch of the Northern Line of the electric Merseyrail network and the non-electrified Manchester-Southport Line, currently operated by Northern Trains. The station reflects its former glory and the trainshed is a fantastic structure: wrought iron columns supporting a glass canopy which enables loads of light to shine through onto the platforms.

The station is well maintained, clean & tidy, with hanging baskets and other floral arrangements to complement the pleasing architectural aesthetics.

The Liverpool line was originally built in 1848 by the Liverpool, Crosby and Southport Railway to a temporary station at Eastbank Street, about half a mile short of the current terminus. The latter opened as Southport Chapel Street in August 1851 and became the terminus for all trains in 1857, when passenger services were transferred from Southport London Street.

In 1904, the line from Liverpool was electrified. The station once boasted 11 platforms, plus two excursion platforms, but now there are only six (Platforms 1-3, with third rail track for Liverpool trains, and Platforms 4, 5 and 6 for Manchester), the rest having been demolished.

(4)	**Southport - Liverpool Central**	**508 127**	**19 miles 00 chains**
	Sandhills - Liverpool Central		2 miles 8 chains
(5)	Liverpool Central - West Kirby	508 130	10 miles 20 chains

West Kirby (above) : *The station is the westernmost terminus on the Wirral Line, which has a central island platform between two terminus tracks, with a siding each side for out-of-use EMUs. The line dates back to the 1870s and was electrified in March 1938 by the London, Midland & Scottish Railway.*

No.508 130 now waits to leave with 2W25, the 12:36hrs 'out & back' circular service via Liverpool. Note, the station concrete platform awning is of Art Deco design, also dating back to the 1930s.

Merseyrail Diary

(6)	West Kirby - Birkenhead North	508 130	6 miles 40 chains

Birkenhead North (above) : "Change here for trains to New Brighton", *which is actually what I did after leaving West Kirby. Behind the station, out of view, is Birkenhead North Traction & Rolling Stock Maintenance Depot (T&RMSD), the main depot for the Merseyrail fleet of EMUs.*

This station replaced an earlier terminus at Wallasey Bridge Road, which opened in 1866, and was originally called Birkenhead Docks, opening in January 1888 as a through station with Birkenhead Park station becoming the new terminus. The old station buildings on Platform 3 can just be glimpsed on the left.

At Bidston East Junction, about half-a-mile west of the station, freight lines ran to the Mersey Docks and Harbour Company, to link with the 'Up' and 'Down' Canning Street lines, 4 miles and 60 chains later, at Rock Ferry. These lines are now out of use, but some readers may remember a time when Class 9f 2-10-0 steam locos worked this route conveying iron ore from Bidston Dock to Shotton steelworks.

New Brighton

This station opened in 1888 as the northern terminus of the Wirral Railway's route from Birkenhead Park station, with through services via the Mersey railway tunnel from Liverpool, following electrification.

Interestingly, between 1960 and 1971, diesel services ran on the 'Borderlands Line' from Wrexham to Bidston, through to New Brighton. However, the last leg from Bidston to New Brighton was little used, as most passengers from the west of the Wirral and North Wales headed for Liverpool. In January 1971, the service became truncated and terminated at Birkenhead North before being cut back further in October 1978 to Bidston.

For the record, I travelled on the 'Borderlands Line' in September 2017 with Class 150 DMU No.150 229 on 2F64, the 13:32 Bidston - Wrexham Central. The half-mile section of track between Wrexham General and Wrexham Central, was the only piece of new track I needed!

(7)	Birkenhead North - New Brighton	507 005	3 miles 00 chains

New Brighton (above) : *Station sign at New Brighton railway station.*

This is a seaside resort forming part of the town of Wallasey, at the northeastern tip of the Wirral peninsula. Although I did not have time to check this out for myself, the town has sandy beaches which look out to the Irish Sea and River Mersey estuary. Plus, it boasts the longest promenade in the UK at just over two miles in length.

The building shown on the sign, at the end of the pier, is Fort Perch Rock. This is a coastal defence battery built between 1825 - 1829, to protect the Port of Liverpool. It was to be a fortified lighthouse to replace the old Perch Rock Light, but a separate lighthouse was built.

(below) : Class 507, 3-car EMU, No.507 005, having brought me in to New Brighton, now stands at Platform 2, ready to depart with 2N29, the 13:23 New Brighton - New Brighton service. This train will travel from and back to New Brighton in a clockwise direction via:

> *James Street, Moorfields, Lime Street, Liverpool Central, James Street.*

There are two sidings adjacent to Platform 1 and Wall siding alongside Platform 2.

(8)   **New Brighton - Liverpool Central**   507 005   **6 miles 60 chains**

Merseyside Distractions

(above) : *This is the Liverpool waterfront, looking across the River Mersey, where the Cunard cruise liner 'Queen Elizabeth' is berthed. Standing behind the ship is the Royal Liver building, located at Pier Head, one of the 'Three Graces". The other two tall buildings are the West Tower (460ft) and the Alexander Tower (289ft).*

(opposite) : *This was my view from Hartley Quay of an interesting and eclectic mix of architectural styles and artifacts. The scene is dominated by the City museum, art gallery and the Royal Liver building, which has a famous 'Liver bird' perched on top of each tower.*

Beneath these structures, are the old Great Western Railway goods shed, used for storage of onward goods received from Birkenhead station, then GWR. Other dockside machinery can also be seen.

(below) : *Large ships, and by this I mean oil tankers, still sail up the Mersey to discharge at Stanlow oil refinery, a little further east of here. MV. 'Nordic Aurora', looking decidedly rusty in places, has these vital statistics:*

Built in 1999   /   899ft in length   /   80,668 gross tonnage   /   summer deadweight of 147,262 tonnes.

Merseyrail Diary

(9)	**Liverpool Central - Kirkby**	**508 139**	**7 miles 40 chains**
	Walton Jct - Kirkby		3 miles 54 chains

Kirkby

Kirkby railway station is like Ormskirk in that it is also a cross-platform interchange between Merseyrail services from Liverpool Central and Northern Trains services from Manchester Victoria via Wigan Wallgate. It is situated seven and a half miles north-east of Liverpool Central and is the operational terminus of both the Kirkby branch of Merseyrail's Northern Line and the Kirkby Branch Line from Wigan.

Historically, the original station was built in 1848, as part of the Liverpool and Bury Railway and consisted of two platforms. After nationalisation in 1948, the use of the line as a through route between Liverpool and Manchester declined, but commuter levels warranted something in the region of 20 trains each way per day.

In 1963, Beeching was prepared to wield the axe and close the line, but his proposals were fortunately rejected by the government in December 1967 and the station became part of a newly created Merseyside Passenger Transport Executive rail network in 1969.

From 1970, the line through the station was singled to reduce track maintenance costs, with the Wigan-bound platform being taken out of use. The station was subsequently rebuilt in 1977, when the line from Liverpool was electrified; electric trains started running in May 1977.

The same year saw the end of through-running between Wigan and Liverpool due to:

a) Liverpool Exchange station closed; new underground stations at Moorfields and Central.
b) DMUs could no longer operate in the new tunnels for safety reasons.

To maintain a through service to the centre of Liverpool, the section from Walton Junction to Kirkby (3 miles and 54 chains) was 750 V DC, third-rail electrified. The remainder of the line to Wigan Wallgate stayed in the hands of diesel multiple units. As a result, Kirkby became the cross-platform interchange station it is today.

(right) : *Class 508 No.508 139 at Kirkby, having arrived with 2K30, the 14:05hrs service from Liverpool Central*

(opposite) : *Looking down the whole length of the platform, you can see Merseyrail EMU No.508 139 in the distance, which is actually on the other side of the B5192 road bridge that bisects the site.*

(below) : *Policemen and station staff keep a watchful eye on proceedings while, at the buffer stop at the end of the non-electrified line, Class 250 No.150 134 waits patiently with 2J66, the 14:44 Kirkby - Blackburn.*

I travelled on this service as far as Manchester Victoria, as I needed the stretch of line from Hindley (Crows Nest Jct.) to Salford Crescent, as well as Kfrom irkby to Wigan Wallgate.

I returned to Wigan Wallgate via one more piece of new line, Lostock Jct - Crows Nest Jct. All in all, a very successful day.

'Fill In Moves'

Kirkby - Wigan Wallgate	150 134	12 miles	7 chains
Crows Nest Jct - Salford Crescent	150 134	13 miles	5 chains
Lostock Jct - Crows Nest Jct	150 110	3 miles	59 chains

Setting The Scene

Between 2016 - 2018, there still remained some 'gaps' in the North West which needed to be done. Most were the odd branch line, here and there, plus a few small sections of track. Some of these were completed at the same time as other sojourns, already detailed, so this is a 'diary' of the missing links.

4th July 2017

Having arrived at Preston (my base for the next few days) on a Voyager, my plan was to enjoy a run to Colne, followed by a return trip with the same DMU right through to Blackpool South, before returning to Preston. Here's the basic details, with all new track shown in red ink, plus the respective mileage.

No.150 419

Preston ------> Blackburn ------> Rose Grove ------> Gannow Jct. ------> Colne	6 miles 38 chains
Colne ------> Rose Grove ------> Blackburn ------> Preston ------> Kirkham & Wesham ------> Blackpool South	12 miles 13 chains

Unfortunately, following my arrival at Blackpool South, there was insufficient time to get a photograph, so I had to make do with a few other images as a record of my journey.

Accrington (left) : *Immediately after the Accrington station stop, the railway makes a tight curve onto Accrington Viaduct, affording good views across the town, especially of the rows of old 'back to back' terraced houses. These dwellings are synonymous with the former East Lancashire milling and textile industry.*

Accrington was the former centre of the cotton and textile machinery industries and is actually famed for manufacturing the hardest and densest building bricks in the world. These were used in the construction of the Empire State Building and the foundations of Blackpool Tower.

Colne (left) : *Here is No.150 419 upon arrival at Colne with 2N14, the 13;20hrs service from Blackpool South.*

The station opened in October 1848, as the terminus of the Leeds and Bradford Extension Railway from Bradford and Skipton. It became an 'end-on' junction with the East Lancashire Railway's Blackburn, Burnley, Accrington and Colne Extension Railway, which opened in February 1849.

The Skipton - Colne section closed in February 1970, although many would like to see it re-open.

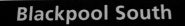

Blackpool (left) : *Blackpool South is the terminus of the South Fylde Line, opened in May 1903 as Waterloo Road before being renamed Blackpool South in March 1932.*

The line is now single track all the way from Kirkham & Wesham and the station consists of a single platform with a bus shelter style structure as the only waiting facilities

(bottom left) : *On the way, my train stopped briefly at Blackpool Pleasure Beach station and I could see the 'Big One', formerly known as the Pepsi Max Big One. This is a steel roller coaster located at Blackpool Pleasure Beach, designed by Ron Toomer and manufactured by Arrow Dynamics, opening to the public in May*

It was the tallest roller coaster in the world until Fujiyama opened at Fuji-Q Highland, Japan, in July 1996.

7th July 2017

Today was all about triangles, two in fact, the first involving Manchester Airport and the other Glossop and Hadfield, which used to form part of the non-standard 'Woodhead' overhead electric system.

My day started off from Preston onboard a Trans-Pennine Express (EMU No.350 405) working 1M91, the 06:15 Edinburgh Waverley - Manchester Airport. I intended to do the two spurs linking the airport terminus with the main line.

No.350 405

Preston ------> Wigan North Western ------> Golborne Jct. ------> Patricroft. ------> Manchester Oxford Road Manchester Piccadilly ------> Slade Lane Jct.------> Heald Green North Jct. ------> Heald Green West Jct. ------> Manchester Airport

1 mile 51 chains

No.323 228

Manchester Airport ------> Heald Green West Jct. ------> Heald Green South Jct. ------> **Wilmslow**

0 miles 38 chains

After completing the run, it was back to Manchester Piccadilly for the next leg.

Manchester Airport

Manchester Airport train station opened at the same time as the second terminal - 1993.

The station is nearly 10-miles from Manchester Piccadilly situated at the end of a short branch from the Styal Line, which in turn is accessed via a triangular junction between Heald Green and Styal stations.

Also, Manchester's 'Metrolink' tram services were extended to the airport in November 2014 and operate to Manchester Victoria.

The Government announced in January 2013, that Manchester Airport would be included in the second phase of 'High Speed 2'.

(top) : *Upon arrival at Manchester Airport, passengers make their way to the airport check-in, while I await my train out of the station.*

(right) : *Looking the other way, Class 323 EMU No.323 228 arrives with 2G14, the 11:18 Manchester Piccadilly - Manchester Piccadilly via Manchester Airport and Crewe.*

I took this unit as far as Wilmslow, to complete the lines serving Manchester Airport from the north and south.

7th July 2017

The Manchester - Glossop Line

This line connects Manchester with the towns of Hadfield and Glossop in Derbyshire.

In December 1984, electrification of the Manchester – Glossop / Hadfield line was converted from 1500 V DC to 25 kV AC. Class 303 EMUs took over from veteran Class 506 EMUs before they later returned to the Glasgow area. These, in turn, were replaced by Class 304s and Class 305s before the incumbent Class 323s were introduced in November 1997.

The line is the surviving section of the famed Woodhead Line, which was electrified in the early 1950s linking Manchester and Sheffield, but passenger services east of Hadfield were withdrawn in 1970, followed by complete closure in 1981. Closure of the Woodhead line was sadly mourned by enthusiasts, myself included, I never had the opportunity to travel over what was one of the most scenic lines in England.

The plan ....

.... was to complete another triangle of lines:

> Dinting West Jct. - Glossop
>
> Glossop - Hadfield
>
> Hadfield - Dinting East Jct. - Dinting West Jct.

As all trains to Hadfield went via Glossop, I assumed (wrongly) that the return from Hadfield would be direct but this was not the case. I soon discovered, on leaving Hadfield, my train went back the same way, so the third part of the triangle was missed.

You would think, after all this time, I would have learnt to check the timetable!

In fact, as I later discovered, some services did return from Hadfield to Manchester direct, mostly during 'peak periods and I revisited the line in September to complete the missing link!

I really enjoyed the 'Glossop line', which passed through some beautiful countryside the nearer the line reached the Pennines, crossing on the way two magnificent viaducts: Broadbottom and Dinting. Dinting is the more famous of the two ....

It crosses Glossop Brook and the A57 road between Manchester and Sheffield, opening in 1844 as part of the original Woodhead Line by the Sheffield, Ashton-under-Lyne and Manchester Railway. The viaduct has been modified a number of times, most notably by the addition of seven brick strengthening piers in 1918 - 1920. There are three sections and the viaduct is 1,200ft in length and 119ft in height - a truly impressive sight and I'm sorry I do not have a photograph in my collection.

The train service I used was:

> 2G14, the 11:18 Manchester Piccadilly - Manchester Piccadilly
>
> *via Glossop - Hadfield - Glossop*

No.323 223

Manchester Piccadilly ------> Ashburys ------> Guide Bridge ------> Guide Bridge West Jct. ------>

Hyde Jct. ------> **Dinting** ------> **Dinting South Jct.** ------> **Glossop** ------> **Hadfield**

7 miles 38 chains

The return journey from Hadfield was the reverse of the outward run, save that I alighted at Guide Bridge to do the Rose Hill Marple branch.

I made a return visit to the North West in September 2017 and completed the missing link between Hadfield - Dinting East Junction - Dinting West Junction. I managed a photograph to record the event which is shown on Page 78.

Hadfield ------> Dinting Est Jct. ------> Dinting ------> Dinting West Jct.   0 miles 69 chains

Glossop

(above) : *Upon arrival at Glossop, there was time for a couple of photographs before the driver changed ends for the run to Hadfield. No.323 223 sits at a very clean and tidy station the with circular 2G14 service to and from Manchester Piccadilly.*

The Friends of Glossop Station was formed in 2002 and are actively involved in the 'station adoption' scheme projects, including the creation of a station garden, painting cast iron railings and arranging floral displays.

Hadfield

(middle) : *'End of the Line'.*

All that acts as a reminder of the former 'Woodhead Route' at Hadfield, is some old and rusting overhead wire stanchions, a buffer stop and a Milepost showing 12 miles and 60 chains.

(right) : *No.323 223 waits to return to Manchester Piccadilly with 2G14, via Glossop.*

Dinting

The railway station is situated on what was the busy Trans-Pennine 'Woodhead Route' via Hadfield and is contained within a triangle of lines bounded by:

Dinting West Junction .... Dinting South Junction .... Dinting East Junction

There is no platform on the curve running between Dinting South and Dinting East Junction, just:

Platform 1 : Hadfield trains   **Platform 2** : Glossop trains

(Dinting West to East Junction)   *(Dinting West to South Junction)*

The signal box on the platform at Dinting Station is a Great Central Railway Company type 5 design with 40 levers. It opened in May 1905 to control the Dinting station triangle replacing three separate boxes at each of the respective junctions. The lever frame was extended to 43 levers by the early 1930s.

(above) : *Railway personnel wait patiently for me to take my photograph, so they can wave No.323 223 away on its journey back to Manchester Piccadilly. Dinting signal box can be seen towards the end of Platform 1.*

7th July 2017

The Rose Hill Marple Branch

Alighting at Guide Bridge for a change of train to take me to Rose Hill Marple, fond memories came flooding back of some enjoyable times spent in the '70s and '80s visiting Guide Bridge stabling point. A time when many classes of locos could be seen, but more of this overleaf.

My train arrived for the run to Rose Hill Marple; two Class 142 'Pacer' units. DMU operation as the branch line off the main line from Manchester Piccadilly to New Mills Central was not electrified.

No. 142 040

Guide Bridge ------> Guide Bridge West Jct. ------> Hyde Jct. ------>Hyde North ------> Hyde Central ------>
Woodley ------> Romiley ------> Marple Wharf Jct. ------> Rose Hill Marple

0 miles 78 chains

Rose Hill Marple

The station opened in August 1869, originally named Marple (Rose Hill), later becoming Rose Hill (Marple), before the current Rose Hill Marple was adopted.

It was originally built on the Macclesfield, Bollington and Marple Railway and there used to be dual tracks and two platforms; the southbound platform has long gone. In January 1970, the route south to Bollington and Macclesfield closed to all traffic, passengers between Macclesfield and Manchester preferring the faster West Coast Main Line route via Stockport.

The line was listed for closure in the 1963 Beeching Report, but survived as there were still high levels of commuter traffic on the line to Manchester Piccadilly.

(above) : *No.142 055 waits at Rose Hill Marple in readiness to work 2H54, the 13:23hrs service to Manchester Piccadilly, the driver of which is quietly sitting on a bench, perhaps contemplating what he was going to do after the end of his shift. No.142 040 led into the station.*

7th July 2017

Guide Bridge

It was built by the Sheffield, Ashton-under-Lyne and Manchester Railway on its new line from Ardwick Junction, near to the Manchester and Birmingham Railway's terminus at Store Street (which is now Manchester Piccadilly) to Sheffield.

It opened as Ashton and Hooley Hill in November 1841 when the line opened as far as Godley Toll Bar. It was renamed Ashton in February 1842, becoming the present day Guide Bridge in July 1845.

The station originally had 4 platforms, but the southern platforms were decommissioned and the tracks lifted in 1984 - 1985 as part of track alterations associated with changing over from 1500 V DC to 25 kV AC working on the Hadfield line. The station buildings were subsequently demolished

The station was also where passenger expresses running to and from Manchester Central on the London Marylebone route, changed loco. Trains would be either steam or electric loco-hauled from Sheffield, and a diesel would take the train the final few miles from Guide Bridge into Manchester and vice versa. The Woodhead Line was busy with goods traffic, especially with coal traffic from South Yorkshire to Lancashire power stations.

Through passenger trains ceased running via Woodhead in January 1970 but Dewsnap sidings and Guide Bridge stabling point were busy until the final closure of the Woodhead Line east of Hadfield in July 1981. Class 76 electric locos along with numerous Class 40s were a frequent sight here.

(above) : 'Pacer' No.142 040 approaches Guide Bridge station with 2R16, the 12:34 Manchester Piccadilly - Rose Hill Marple service. The line to the left leads to Heaton Norris Junction and Stockport, a former London & North Western Railway main line between Crewe and Leeds via Stockport, dating back to the 1840s. The line is ostensibly 'freight only' and a diversionary route, seeing only two passenger trains a week, one in each direction on a Saturday morning between Stockport and Stalybridge, serving Denton and Reddish South.

In 2018/19, Denton was deemed the least used station in Great Britain, tied with Stanlow & Thornton with Reddish South ranked the third least used with just 60 entries and exits recorded for the whole year.

This type of service is also known as a 'Parliament' train, operated to comply with the 1844 Railway Regulation Act, which required train companies to provide inexpensive and basic rail transport for less affluent passengers. Although no longer a legal requirement, the term does describe a train service that continues to be run to avoid the cost of formal closure of a route or station.

"Past & Present"

(right) : *Forgive me for choosing a photograph from the first 'Chasing Trains', but this one illustrates the former track layout to the east of the station to good effect.*

Class 40 No.40055 pulls a lengthy rake of 2-axle ballast / spoil wagons out of the sidings. (02/79)

(middle) : *It's New Year's day and a snowy one at that, but a little snow didn't deter intrepid trainspotters!*

Five Class 40s are visible, with No.40082 leading a row of four and No.40169 stabled on its own. Some Class 76 electric locos were also noted on the stabling point. (01/80)

(below) : *Guide Bridge, as it is now, looking east with just two main running lines. The stabling point used to be situated on the right, just beyond the footbridge..*

The lines diverging to the right, are the former Woodhead lines to Hadfield, although my train will leave these at Hyde Junction, for the run via Romiley to reach my destination.

The other lines (diverging to the left) lead to ballast stockpile sidings and through lines to Stalybridge.

22nd September 2017

"Tying Up Loose Ends"

Hunts Cross

A bit of a trek really today, after leaving Preston early morning, simply to cover four, relatively short, sections of track, one of which (Hadfield - Dinting) has been covered previously. I started by completing the missing link in the 'Merseyrail' system ....

No.507 005

Sandhills ------> Moorfields ------> Liverpool Lime St. ------> **Liverpool Central** ------> **St. Michaels** ------>

Liverpool South Parkway ------> **Hunts Cross West Jct.** ------> **Hunts Cross**

7 miles 05 chains

(left) : *Class 507 EMU No.507 005 has arrived at the southern limit of the 'Northern Line' of the Merseyrail system, with 2U21, the 10:43 Southport - Hunts Cross.*

The driver is seen walking up the platform to take No.507 000 with me on board back to Liverpool Central, which forms 2S24, the 11:51hrs train service back to Southport.

Upon arriving at Liverpool Central, I changed trains to catch another EMU (No.507 001) which took me as far as Bidston, where I alighted to do the next leg of my excursion.

A brief incursion into Wales.

Wrexham General

The line between Bidston and Wrexham is known today as the 'Borderlands Line'.

The southern section was built by the Wrexham, Mold and Connah's Quay Railway (WMCQR) in 1864 and the northern part by the North Wales & Liverpool Railway, a joint committee of the WMCQR and the Manchester, Sheffield & Lincolnshire Railway in 1896.

Although I had travelled through the other station in Wrexham (General), I had not been to the other one, simply because I had never been close by to do it. Wrexham Central is the southern terminus of the Borderlands Line, also known as the Wrexham - Bidston line, and the current station was constructed in 1998, replacing the first Central station, which opened in November 1887.

Bidston ------> Bidston Dee Jct. ------> Hawarden Bridge ------> Shotton ------> Penyffordd ------>

Wrexham Exchange Jct. ------> **Wrexham General** ------> **Wrexham Central**

0 miles 52 chains

(left) : *Journey's end - Wrexham Central.*

Class 150 2-car 'Sprinter' No.150 229 is seen 'on the blocks' after arriving with 2J61, the 12:32 Bidston - Wrexham Central.

I travelled back with the same unit as far as Wrexham General, where I caught a Class 175 unit working an ATW service from Cardiff Central to Holyhead. This took me as far as Chester, from where the next leg would begin.

Mickle Trafford - Mouldsworth

A little bit of single line track between these two points on the Chester - Manchester Piccadilly line, via Northwich and Altrincham, was all that's needed!

However, there was no easy way to do this, simply going to Mouldsworth and back to Chester was not practical (time-wise), which meant an 'all stations' stopping train to Manchester Piccadilly would have to do. This would take a further 30 minutes compared to the more direct route.

I had only once travelled on the line (eastbound) via Northwich, but that was back in the 1980s on a railtour when Class 40 No.40192 traversed the 'freight only' line from West Cheshire Junction to Mouldsworth, which has long since closed.

No.150 112

Chester ------> Mickle Trafford Jct. ------> Mouldsworth ------> Northwich ------> Altrincham ------> Gateley ------> Stockport ------> **Manchester Piccadilly**

4 miles 33 chains

~~~~~~

Ordsall Chord

Actually, this record did not happen in September 2017 but, in April 2018, after I visited the "40s @ 60" Gala at the East Lancashire Railway, which I must say was absolutely fabulous (an account is contained in the first "Chasing Trains".

Having travelled on the Manchester 'Metro' from Bury to Manchester Victoria, I had the opportunity to get to Piccadilly station for my train home, via the new Ordsall Chord, which I took.

Ordsall Chord is a short railway line in Ordsall, Salford, which links Manchester Piccadilly and Manchester Oxford Road to Manchester Victoria, designed to increase capacity and reduce journey times into and through Manchester.

In January 2016, Network Rail began work on the foundations. The plan proposed avoiding the Stephenson Bridge and cross the River Irwell on a network arch bridge but, in doing so, severed the Museum of Science and Industry in Manchester's main-line rail connection immediately to the east of the bridge.

The 600-tonne network arch was lifted into place on 21st February 2017 and the first passenger service was at 08:40hrs on 10th December 2017, a service from Manchester Victoria to Manchester Oxford Road followed by a return to Leeds.

Due to the curvature of the new chord, it was difficult obtaining a reasonable shot of the new bridge, which would have to wait until a later date.

No.155 345

Manchester Victoria ------> Manchester Victoria West Jct ------> Deal Street Jct. ------> Salford Central ------> Irwell Bridge Jct. ------> Water Street Jct. ------> Castlefield Jct. ------> Deansgate ------> **Manchester Oxford Road**

<div align="right">1 mile 1 chain</div>

(above) : *Network arch bridge over the River Irwell on the Ordsall Chord.*

23rd September 2017

"A Tale of Four Curves"

Halifax

The day starts off, as usual, from Preston, but this time it's a really enjoyable jaunt, taking in some beautiful countryside, architecture, not forgetting some new track, as I moved through East Lancashire to West Yorkshire.

I had previously only travelled over the Copy Pit route once before, in September 1982 (35 years ago!) westbound with No.40077 on a railtour, so I was looking forward to the ride this time. Just over four miles later after leaving Gannow Junction, the line breasts Copy Pit summit, at 749ft above sea level, not the highest by any means. However, over half of the route is steeper than 1 in 70 and in steam days, freight trains needed assistance to get over the top, with banking assistance being provided by a Class 8f 2-8-0 steam loco off Rose Grove shed.

At Hall Royd Junction, the line joins the Calder Valley route, which is one of my favourites. Thence, to Milner Royd Junction, where my train diverged onto new track via Halifax, where there was time to get a photograph of the signal box, before moving on into Bradford Interchange station.

At Bradford Interchange station, I had a cup of coffee, while my friend Michael took some time out to do a spot of bus spotting at the adjacent bus station, before we set off on the next leg of our journey.

No.158 752

Preston ------> Bamber Bridge ------> Blackburn ------> Accrington ------> Gannow Jct. ------> Copy Pit ------>

Hall Royd Jct. ------> Hebden Bridge ------> Mytholmroyd ------> Sowerby Bridge ------> Milner Royd Jct.

------> Dryclough Jct. ------> Halifax ------> Mill Lane Jct. ------> **Bradford Interchange**

10 miles 61 chains

Bradford Interchange

This is one of two stations in Bradford, the other is Bradford Forster Square - a 10-minute walk away - which mainly uses Class 333 EMUs on the Airedale Line to Skipton, the Wharfedale Line to Ilkley and the Leeds - Bradford Line.

Historically, the original railway station here, named Bradford Exchange, was opened by the Lancashire and Yorkshire Railway and the Great Northern Railway in May 1850. In 1867, the Leeds, Bradford and Halifax Junction Railway, which served Bradford Adolphus station, built a link to Exchange station to join the two existing companies; Adolphus station closed as a result.

The railway station was completely rebuilt on the same site in 1880 with 10 bay platforms and two arched roofs, constructed of wrought iron, resting on a combination of plain stone walls and classical Corinthian style columns down the middle. Glass covered the middle section.

Bringing the story up to date, by 1973, the railway station was considered too large and was rebuilt, a little further south; the old Exchange station was demolished and a new 'Interchange' (linking bus and trains) was designed in 1962 and opened in January 1973. The next two legs:

No.144 016

Bradford Interchange ------> Mill Lane Jct. ------> Halifax ------> Dryclough Jct. ------> Greetland Jct. ------>

Brighouse ------> Bradley Wood Jct. ------> Bradley Jct. ------> Deighton ------> **Huddersfield**

2 miles 28 chains

Leaving Huddersfield, a Class 185 DMU, No.185 102, got us to Manchester Victoria station, so we could complete the last leg of the day's events - the new 'Todmorden Curve'. Beforehand, there was sufficient time to reminisce and investigate the 'new' Victoria station.

In 2009, Victoria was regarded as one of the worst railway stations in the country because of its dilapidated structure and environment. Refurbishment work began in April 2013, the old roof was dismantled that autumn and a new £17 million roof began to be installed in May 2014. The station upgrade was completed in August 2015 and OHLE was installed in 2015.

(above) : *Following an upgrade of the Calder Valley line in 2017, Halifax signal box closed when control of the upgraded track layout and new signalling passed to York Rail Operating Centre in October 2018.*

Originally known as Halifax East 'box, it is located by the 'Down' main line and was fitted with a 52 lever Railway Signal Company Limited frame, which opened in 1885 for the Lancashire & Yorkshire Railway Company, replacing a late 1870s signal box. The lever frame was eventually extended to 54 levers and the original locking was replaced by tappet locking in 1892.

The signal box was renamed Halifax in March 1969, when the lever frame was replaced by a British Railways Eastern Region individual function switch panel, which allowed for the closure of Halifax West signal box.

(below) : *2-car 'Pacer' No.144 016 sits at platform 3, having arrived from Selby with 2W75, the 12:54 Selby - Huddersfield and this will be my train to Huddersfield, taking in two new curves:* **Dryclough Junction to Greetland Junction**, *on to the Calder Valley main line, followed by the curve between* **Bradley Wood Junction to Bradley Junction** *to join the main line between Leeds and Manchester, via Diggle.*

BRADFORD INTERCHANGE

(left) : *This is the view looking south, down the platforms, towards the neck of Bradford Interchange station.*

A 2-car Class 158 Express Unit + 2-car Class 144 'Pacer' formation are about to enter Platform 4 with 1B25, the 11:57 Leeds - Preston service, which will reverse here and depart for Lancashire via Halifax, Copy Pit and Blackburn. The leading vehicle is No.158 843 which sports Northern Trains livery of blue with purple and light blue stripes.

(middle) : *Two fine examples of buffer stops at the end of Platform 3 and Platform 4, respectively.*

MANCHESTER VICTORIA

(below) : *The new Victoria station has been completely modernised and the old dilapidated canopies over the platforms have now gone.*

However, I was pleased to see that some 'finer' aspects of the old Victoria remained, like this superb tiled wall map illustrating the sphere of the former Lancashire & Yorkshire Railway network.

Todmorden Curve

The first trains in 40 years to travel on the 'Todmorden Curve' did so on 17th May 2015, marking the completion of a much-delayed £10m project to provide a direct link between Manchester and Blackburn via Burnley. This new curve would shave 30-minutes off a journey to Blackburn.

I travelled over this new curve aboard 2J64, the 13:44 Kirkby - Blackburn.

No.150 117

Manchester Victoria ------> Thorpes Bridge Jct. ------> Castleton ------> Rochdale ------> Todmorden ------>

Stansfield Hall Jct. ------> Copy Pit ------> Burnley Manchester Road ......> Accrington ------> Blackburn

0 miles 35 chains

We travelled on a Class 158 unit (No.158 859) back to Preston, from where Michael made his way to Blackpool for the evening, while I went on to Carnforth to meet up with my good friend and business colleague, Mark Rawlinson. In doing so, I enjoyed a six-mile thrash with a Class 37 (No.37422) from Lancaster to Carnforth, which was working 2C31, the 17:31 Lancaster - Barrow in Furness.

~~~~~~~~~~~~~~~~~~~~~~~~~~~~~~~~~~~~~

(right) : *On Saturday evening, I spent an enjoyable evening with Mark and his wife Jane, having dinner at a delightful restaurant, accompanied by a couple of rather large glasses of red wine, I might add.*

Class 37/4 No.37422 waits for the off at Lancaster's Platform 5 with train 2C31 to whisk me off on a 6 mile and 20 chains trip to Carnforth.

(right) : *The famous romantic drama film 'Brief Encounter' was partly filmed at Carnforth station in February 1945 and the station clock became a powerful icon through repeated use in the film.*

The film's main stars were Celia Johnson and Trevor Howard, plus Stanley Holloway and Joyce Carey. The screenplay by Noël Coward was based on his 1936 one-act play 'Still Life' and the soundtrack features the Piano Concerto No. 2 by Sergei Rachmaninoff.

24th September 2017

"A Pilgrimage to Blackpool"

I knew the Preston - Blackpool North line would soon be electrified, which would result in the semaphore signalling at Blackpool North station being replaced by modern colour lights controlled from the WCML North Rail Operating Centre in Manchester. The existing station platform layout would also be altered with the eight curved platforms reduced to six and on a straighter alignment.

To carry out this work, a planned station closure would be effected between 1st January 2018 and 16th April 2018, when the station and line re-opened. So, I decided to visit Blackpool North and take some photographs of the famous signals and, at the same time, sample the heritage trams, which would be out and about on the Sunday working the promenade between Blackpool and Fleetwood.

As Blackpool North is effectively a 'closed station', passengers are only allowed on to a platform when a train is ready to depart, I had to first seek permission to take photographs. This I duly did and was given an orange High Visibility Jacket to wear for health & safety purposes.

(left) : *Class 150 225 slows as it brings 1N80, the 16:12 Liverpool Lime Street - Blackpool North service into the Lancashire terminus, sandwiched between two semaphore signals. Each one has a 'Home' (red arm with vertical white stripe) and a 'Distant (yellow with black vee-stripe) signal, plus a small 'arml' for shunting purposes.*

The only difference between the two is that one signal is mounted on a metal post, the one a concrete post.

(below) : *Class 156 No.156 443 brings up the rear of a 2 x 2-car formation, which is leaving with 1B38, the 17:17 Blackpool North - York, via Blackburn, Copy Pit and Halifax.*

Blackpool North No.2 signal box closed at 02:31hrs on 11th November 2017 and was demolished 3 - 4 days later.

(above) : *No.84 signal (Platform 6 Starting) and No.85 signal (Platform 5 Starting) are mounted on a British Railways London Midland Region two doll balanced bracket on a tubular steel post. The signal has been fitted with modern staging with strong handrails.*

(overleaf) : **"The Twilight Hour'** *.... a panoramic sweep of the station, showing all the signals controlling the departures from Blackpool North station along with the curvature of the platforms*

24th September 2017

Blackpool Trams

"A day at the seaside", well, actually an enjoyable day riding the Blackpool Tramway between Blackpool to Fleetwood for the first time, a stretch of 11-miles. The line dates back to 1885 and is one of the oldest electric tramways in the world, operated by Blackpool Transport.

The tramway initially used a 'Conduit' system, whereby trams took electricity from a conduit below and between the tracks, until 1899 when 550 V overhead wiring was installed and the conduit removed. Trams run from Starr Gate in the south of Blackpool to Fleetwood, but in busy periods such as during Blackpool Illuminations, start or terminate short at Cleveleys, Little Bispham, Bispham or the Pleasure Beach to allow a more intensive service through the centre of Blackpool.

Heritage Trams

Blackpool has an extensive range of their own trams retained from yesteryear, as well as some from other locations, which are now operated as Blackpool Heritage Tram Tours. Most sport traditional green and cream livery of BTS from the 1930s to the 1990s, some in red and cream/white, plus some others carrying colourful all-over advertisements.

The Heritage Trams are often out & about during summer weekends and I purchased a Heritage Day Ticket and here are some of the images I captured during the day. A wonderful experience.

('Balloon' No.713) : *Blackpool Pleasure Beach*

These 'Balloon' trams were built by English Electric in 1934 - 1935, of which the first thirteen were open-topped and the remaining fourteen enclosed. They were numbered 237–263, but re-numbered in 1968 becoming Nos. 700–726. Various all-over adverts have since appeared on several 'Balloon' tramcars.

No.713 was originally No.250 when built in 1935.

(previous page) : **(Bolton No.66)** : *Blackpool Promenade*

Car 66 was built in 1901 for Bolton Corporation by Electric Railway and Tramway Carriage Works of Preston. It was originally an open topper and was later fitted with a top deck cover, followed by enclosed top deck ends.

It was withdrawn towards the end of the Bolton system in 1946 (right) : **No.40**

Blackpool Pleasure Beach

Blackpool & Fleetwood 'Box' No.40 was originally built for the Blackpool & Fleetwood Tramroad Company in 1914.

It is an example of a closed saloon tramcar and had a working life in Blackpool until 1936 when it was withdrawn

(middle) :

No.737 'Fishing Trawler'

Blackpool Promenade

'The Trawler', No.737, is based on the design of the Fleetwood fishing trawler. It was originally, Brush car No.633, new as No.296 in 1937 which forms its base.

Initially, it kept fleet number No.633, but was renumbered in the Feature Car series as No.737 in 2008.

(below) :

Old & New alike at Blackpool North Pier - 'Three For the Price of One'

Bombardier Flexity 2 No.009
'Bolton' No.66
'Balloon' No.711

('Brush Car' No.623) : *Blackpool Pleasure Beach*

Built in Loughborough, Brush car No.286 entered service in July 1937 and received several modifications over the years, losing its sliding roof panels in 1964 and the roof windows were panelled over in 1973. At the same time, the twin destination blinds were replaced with a single indicator. No.286 was renumbered to No.623 in 1968.

('Brush Car' No.631) : *Blackpool Promenade*

This tram was built in August 1937 as one of 20 single deck streamlined 'Railcoaches' (284 – 303) supplied by the Brush Electrical Engineering Co., Loughborough. The Brush cars survived the contraction of the tramway in the 1960's largely intact and in 1968 the surviving eighteen were renumbered, becoming Nos.621 – 638.

('Open Boat' No.600) : *Blackpool Pleasure Beach*

This is the prototype of 12 open boat cars built by English Electric in 1934 as part of General Manager Walter Luff's five year modernisation plan, which saw 116 new trams supplied during the 1930's. Three prototypes were constructed of different designs with No.225 delivered in January 1934. It became No.600 in 1968.

(inset) : *Blackpool Corporation Transport crest.*

('Balloon' 723) : *Blackpool Promenade*

SCOTTISH BRANCHES
18th September to 21st September 2018

Background

This particular 'track bashing' outing was one of my favourites, great fun, even though all the lines I set out to cover were only worked by either ScotRail DMUs or EMUs.

I arrived in Scotland via the WCML, having already purchased a 'Spirit of Scotland' rail rover, valid for any four days in a seven day period. This ticket represented excellent value at just £91.75, taking into account a third-off discount with my Senior railcard.

For my stay in Scotland, I based myself at a Holiday Inn, situated in West Nile Street in the centre of Glasgow; Glasgow Queen Street station was only a five minute walk away and Glasgow Central a further 5 minutes.

Real Time Trains and My Mobile

Before I left Swindon, I had already mapped out my itinerary for each day, making the best use of time to achieve my objectives. Details of the journeys made each day are set out in the next few pages and the 'required' track is annotated in red.

How times have changed, I recall having to carry around with me the cumbersome and heavy 'All Systems Timetable', which was the only complete reference for train travel on British Railways. Nowadays, all this timetable information (and more) is set out in a simple application (App.) called Real Time Trains (RTT) which is held on my Apple Iphone and accessible at just a simple click on the app. Not only that, it's free!

Using this data, it enabled me to check each journey as I travelled from one station to another and see if any of my planned services were delayed, or even cancelled, which did prove to be the case on several occasions during my stay.

The App. enabled me to quickly change my plans 'on the go' and establish the best way to maintain my schedule, especially when there were 'tight' connections to be made. On the whole, the week panned out to my expectations, except that I did lose one day's travel due to reasons beyond my control, which I will come onto later.

RTT is an extremely invaluable tool providing up-to-date 'real time' train information, without which it would not have been possible to undertake the journeys I made, without wasting a considerable amount of time revising my schedule - thank you, RTT.

Day 1

By the time I arrived in Scotland and checked-in to my hotel, it was late afternoon and the light was fading fast. I decided to make a short trip to get the first new track 'in the book', before I called it a day to relax over a nice meal and enjoy a glass of red wine, or two!

The required track basically involved a loop from Glasgow Queen Street Low level station and back to Glasgow Queen Street High Level, necessitating a change of train at Springburn.

I left the Low Level station behind Class 318 EMU No.318 265 on a service to Cumbernauld, which enabled me to travel over the line linking Bellgrove and Springburn.

At Springburn, I waited for the train from Falkirk Graham Street to arrive (Class 170 No.170 471 (*left*)), which would take me back into the main Glasgow Queen Street station via a single line spur from Sighthill West Junction to Cowlairs South junction.

Tuesday, 18th September 2018		
Loco / Unit	**Journey Made**	**Train Reporting Details**
318 265	Glasgow Queen St. - Springburn	2V46, 17:56 Dumbarton Central - Cumbernauld
	Bellgrove - Duke St - Barnhill - Sighthill East Jct	
170 471	Springburn - Glasgow Queen St	2J77, 18:22 Falkirk Graham St - Glasgow Queen St
	Sighthill West Jct - Cowlairs South Jct	

Day 2

Setting the Scene

This proved to be a day to remember where the weather had a major impact and resulted, for the most part, with my plans for the day being shelved. Torrential rain and gale force winds threatened to hit the west of Scotland late morning onwards - this was **Storm Ali**.

The plan was to go to Largs, with a quick trip to East Kilbride beforehand.

East Kilbride is situated at the end of a non-electrified line off the main line to Kilmarnock at Busby Junction.

The branch is 7 miles and 60 chains long and after reaching Busby, the line continues as single track for the remaining four miles to East Kilbride.

On arrival, I dashed out into the pouring rain to snatch a record of my visit, hauled by Class 156

DMU No.156 465 (right). This car formed part of a 2-car set and I sat in No.156 456 for the run back to Glasgow.

Back at Central station, it was a relatively quick turnround and catch my train to Largs.

Going to Largs

Largs is on the Firth of Clyde in North Ayrshire, about 33 miles from Glasgow, 42 miles by train. It is a popular seaside resort with a pier and has historic links with the Vikings. In 1263 it was the site of the Battle of Largs between the Norwegian and the Scottish armies. The original name means "the slopes" (An Leargaidh) in Scottish Gaelic.

I left the Glasgow terminus on the 09:48hrs service to Largs in the hands of a relatively new and modern Siemens Class 380 'Desiro' EMU, operated by Abellio ScotRail on services in the Ayrshire and Inverclyde region of Scotland . A total of 38 Class 380 sets were ordered, comprising 22 three-car and 16 four-car units. Stations along the Ayrshire Coast Line and Inverclyde Line underwent platform extension work to cater for longer trains.

At Kilwinning Junction, my train waited for several minutes for a path onto the branch serving Ardrossan and Largs. This was to be a foretaste of what was to come, as trains had started to be delayed due to the inclement weather. In fact, where the line runs close to the sea at Saltcoats, it was clear that winds were strengthening with waves crashing over the sea wall and onto my train.

Glasgow Central

(above) : *This is the west end of Glasgow Central with Platforms 15, 14, 13 and 12 in view; the first two housing two sets of Class 380 EMUs awaiting their next turns of duty. No.380 011 has arrived with 1T06, the 08:33 service from Largs while No.380 017 waits to leave with my train, 1T07, the 09:48hrs departure to Largs.*

Saltcoats

(below) : *This is the view looking through the carriage window as No.380 017 made its way beside the sea wall between Saltcoats and Ardrossan South Beach. This shot is the best I could achieve and doesn't really capture the wild and stormy conditions lashing the railway at this point.*

Largs

(above) : *Braving the elements .... detraining at Largs, I just had to try and record the scene - gloominess, gale force winds and driving rain sweeping across the platform as I tried to keep the camera steady and dry. You can just about see the force of the rain, as No.380 017 stands forlorn, its duties done for the day.*

Storms regularly batter South West Scotland and, for the record, between 1981 - 2010 the average annual rainfall in Largs was 53 inches, eight inches more than UK national average.

(below) : *The well kept garden alongside Platform 2 at Largs railway station in the gloom, part of Scotrail's 'Adopt a Station' scheme - see overleaf for more details.*

Storm Ali

Upon reaching Largs, I stepped onto the platform and was nearly blown over by the strength of the wind and driving rain - I have never experienced anything like it with winds reaching 100mph - Storm Ali had arrived with a vengeance.

The weather became so bad that ScotRail curtailed all services running in and out of Largs for the foreseeable future - due to fallen trees on the line and damaged OHLE - a decision which was reflected pretty well everywhere in Scotland and northern England. Thousands were left without power, or faced severe travel disruption, while, in south-west Scotland, children were banned from walking home from school because of the risk of injury from flying debris.

So, what now .....I was stuck in Largs of all places and I needed to get back to Glasgow.

Largs - After The Storm

The rain had stopped falling, the winds had died down and even the sun decided to put in an appearance.

However, this was deceptive as the damage caused by Storm Ali had already taken its toll and no more trains were running today.

(left) : What a difference an hour or so makes, No.380 017 sits in Platform 2 which will have to wait until the morning to work back to Glasgow.

Largs - 'Adopt a Station'

The new community garden was created by local group 'Largs Organic Garden' as part of ScotRail's 'Adopt a station' programme, and includes flowers, plants, a path which is fully accessible for wheelchairs, and the bow of a Viking long boat *(see below)*. The project took 12 weeks to complete from design to finish with many of the supplies and labour donated in kind by local trade businesses.

More than 275 ScotRail stations across the country are part of the 'Adopt a Station' programme.

Eventually, *Storm Ali* moved further east and a sense of calm, even some sunshine, prevailed over Largs. But, the damage had already been done and Network Rail had the onerous task of clearing the lines and repairing OHLE in the hope that a normal train service could resume the following day.

I did mention to a member of the station staff that I had never experienced such adverse weather conditions, but I was told this was common in this part of Scotland!

The next question I faced was how to get back to Glasgow?

No trains were running. Even the local bus services weren't running to anything resembling normal service and, if they were, it was about a two hour run to Glasgow. There were other rail passengers with more important needs than mine; one had to get to Edinburgh Airport for a flight, others with connecting rail tickets to other parts of the rail network.

A partial solution ....

Largs is out on a limb and the nearest station with any connections to the north or south is Kilwinning, 16 miles away.

To help stranded passengers, a 'rail-replacement' bus service to Kilwinning was laid on using a single decker coach *(right)*, commandeered off a school run.

It retraced the itinerary of the train service, calling at the following railway stations:

- Fairlie

- West Kilbride

- Ardrossan South Beach   - Saltcoats   - Steventon

Arriving at Kilwinning railway station about one hour later, all four platforms had Class 380 units parked up, but going nowhere.

"Taxi"

In the station forecourt, I noticed a taxi driver sitting in the driver's seat and asked if he was available for business.

He told me he was and I asked for a fare to Glasgow - £50 but, as he had to go to Glasgow today in any event, he would only charge me £40 and I gladly accepted his kind offer.

The journey was slower than normal, having to avoid fallen trees and branches on the road. Apart from seeing similar incidents on the television news bulletins, this (fortunately) proved to be the only time I have witnessed a parked car crushed by a fallen tree.

During the journey, we enjoyed some friendly conversation and as we were both ardent football fans, football was the main topic of conversation.

Back in Glasgow

My ride dropped me back outside Glasgow Central station and, after a brief inspection I made my way across the City to Glasgow Queen Street station. The only trains running here was a shuttle service to Anniesland and back. As I required the single line spur from Maryhill to Anniesland, I decided to do this and at least get a little something extra out of what was a disappointing day.

The net result of this debacle was that I effectively lost the best part of a day's schedule and had to 'shoehorn' my schedule into the remaining three days of my visit to Scotland.

Hopefully, Network Rail would get the railway up and running again by the morning!

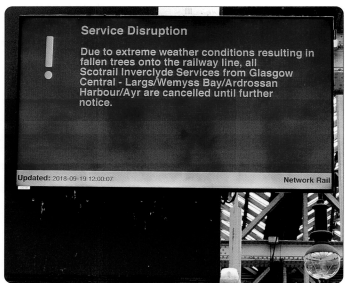

Glasgow Central

(left) : This was the message being displayed at Glasgow Central on Tuesday, 19th September, after Storm Ali had wreaked chaos on the rail network.

Anniesland

(below) : *It's only a journey of 5 miles and 36 chains, taking 20 minutes to complete, and a half-hourly service operates between Glasgow Queen Street and Anniesland.*

Class 156 No.156442, stands in the bay at Anniesland having arrived with 2W57 from Glasgow Queen Street. It will now form 2W56 return.

The section (74 chains) from here to Maryland Park Junction is single track and not electrified.

Wednesday, 19th September 2018		
156 465	Glasgow Central - East Kilbride	2J04, 08:15 Glasgow Central - East Kilbride
	Eglington St Jct - Muirhouse Central Jct	
	Busby Jct - East Kilbride	
156 456	East Kilbride - Glasgow Central	2J05, 08:57 East Kilbride - Glasgow Central
380 017	Glasgow Central - Largs	1T07, 09:48 Glasgow Central - Largs
	Ardrossan South Beach - Largs	
156 442	Glasgow Queen St - Anniesland	2W57, 13:56 Glasgow Queen St - Anniesland
	Maryhill Central Jct - Anniesland	
156 442	Anniesland - Glasgow Queen St	2W56, 14:21 Anniesland - Glasgow Queen St

Glasgow Central
Normal Service is resumed

(above) : This is the view of the concourse at Glasgow Central, 06:30hrs in the morning, the day after the storm and a departure board displaying a full complement of services, pretty well back to normal, save for some delays on Ayrshire coast services. The concourse is, however, rather unusually devoid of commuters!

(below) : That's more like it, trains running as usual. The main purpose of this image is to show the signal gantry at the south end of the station controlling all departures. The famous '20mph ALL LINES' speed restriction is prominently placed on the gantry.

Class 320 EMU No.320 321 is seen leaving the terminus with 2N34, the 17:37 to Neilston while, a little further out, Class 380 No.380 106 makes its way across the network of points with 1F72 to Largs.

Day 3

The Plan

After a hearty breakfast - and I must confess that I really do enjoy starting the day with a full 'English' - I made my way over to Glasgow Central station to see what was going on, hopefully there would be no disruption to the schedule I had planned for Wednesday.

It was to be a full day to take in the following lines and branches I needed to cover, which were:

> Neilston
>
> Larkhall
>
> Milngavie
>
> Balloch
>
> Helensburgh Central
>
> Lanark

To complete the itinerary; a short spur linking Cathcart North Junction with King's Park.

The Day Itself

Fortunately, services were back to normal and, suffice to say, the itinerary worked like clockwork, starting off with a local service from Glasgow Central to Neilston and culminating back in Central station off the 17:19hrs service from Newton.

I had planned to go over to Edinburgh on both the 20th and 21st to sample the two evening DRS Class 68 loco-hauled services on the 'Fife Circle' but, due to the setback following 'Storm Ali' the day before, I only had time for one evening.

There were many highlights and I particularly enjoyed the new branches that I visited along with a run via Glasgow Central Low Level, a day starting from Glasgow Central station and finishing back there some 10 hours later.

I will let some images tell the story of the day ....

Glasgow Central Low Level

One of the highlights for me was using the lines through the Low level station, which I did in its entirety using a service from Larkhall to Milngavie - see Page 106 for details.

The low-level platforms were originally a two island separate station to serve the underground Glasgow Central Railway, which opened in August 1896. This railway was taken over by the Caledonian Railway in 1890; services ran from Maryhill Central and from the Lanarkshire & Dunbartonshire Railway in the west through to Rutherglen, Carmyle, Newton, and other Caledonian Railway destinations to the east of Glasgow.

Of particular interest are the series of tunnels between Dalmarnock and Exhibition Centre, which run for three miles, east to west:

Tunnel	M. Ch.
1. Dalmarnock Road	0. 36
2. Canning Street	0. 21
3. Anderston	1. 46
4. Stobcross Street	0. 29

Interestingly, eastbound services (only) go through Kelvinhaugh Tunnel (29 chains) between Finnieston West Junction and Exhibition Centre.

Neilston (above) : *Having arrived in Neilston on platform 2, Class 320 No.320 306 moved into the headshunt, a further 14 chains to the end of the line, beyond the red signal, to reverse and transfer to the nearside platform 1, ready to work back to Glasgow Central (2N15) at 08:43hrs.*

Larkhall (below) : *Class 318 No.318 250 is seen 'on the blocks' at Larkhall station after arriving with 2L16, the 09:18 hrs service from Dalmuir.*

The station was originally opened as Larkhall Central in July 1905 by the Caledonian Railway as part of their Mid Lanark Lines but closed to passengers in October 1965. Forty years after closure, the station was officially reopened on 9 December 2005 by Jack McConnell MSP, the then First Minister for Scotland.

Day 3

Best Run of the Day   2L19, the 10:33 Larkhall - Milngavie

M. Ch.	Location	Arr.	Dep.	
0. 00	**LARKHALL**		**10:33**	Service off **2L16** from Dalmuir
0. 59	Merryton	10:35	10:35	
2. 05	Allanton Loop	pass		
2. 26	Chatelherault	10:38	10:38	
2. 74	Haughhead Jct.	pass		
4. 13	Hamilton central	10:42	10:42	
5. 04	Hamilton West	10:45	10:45	
6. 67	Blantyre	10:48	10:48	
9. 58	Newton	10:52	10:52	
10. 33	Newton West Jct	pass		
11. 25	Cambuslang	10:56	10:56	
12. 42	Rutherglen East Jct	pass		
12. 78	Rutherglen Central Jct	pass		
13. 11	Rutherglen	11:00	11:00	
13. 24	Rutherglen North Jct	pass		
13. 74	Dalmarnock	11:03	11:03	
14. 34	Bridgeton	11:05	11:05	
15. 53	Argyle Street	11:08	11:08	
16. 01	**GLASGOW CENTRAL**	**11:09**	**11:09**	
16. 35	Anderston	11:11	11:11	
16. 76	Exhibition Centre	11:13	11:13	
17. 34	Finnieston East Jct	pass		
17. 67	Finnieston West Jct	pass		
18. 13	Partick	11:16	11:16	
18. 69	Hyndland	11:18	11:19	
19. 16	Hyndland East Jct	pass		
19. 40	Hyndland North Jct	pass		
19. 64	Anniesland	11:22	11:22	
21. 10	Westerton	11:25	11;25	
22. 21	Bearsden	11:28	11;28	
22. 66	Hillfoot	11:30	11:30	
24. 35	**MILNGAVIE**	**11:33**		forms **2C30** service to Cumbernauld

Notes :

Pronunciations :

Town	Scottish	Scottish Gaelic
Cambuslang	Cammuslang	Camas Lang
Milngavie	Mulguye	Muileann-Gaidh

Chatelherault is derived from the French town of Châtellerault, the title Duc de Châtellerault granted to James Hamilton, 2nd Earl of Arran in 1548 for his part in arranging the marriage of Mary, Queen of Scots, to Francis, the Dauphin of France.

Diagram :

The full diagram for No.318 250 is shown on the opposite page, which shows how intensive suburban services are in the Strathclyde area.

Day 3

Full Daily Diagram for No.318 250

Headcode	Train Reporting Details		
5R08	**06:20**	**Yoker C. S.**	**Dalmuir**
2R08	06.33	Dalmuir	Whifflet
5S11	07:30	Whifflet	Whifflet
2S11	08:02	Whifflet	Dalmuir
2L16	09:20	Dalmuir	Larkhall
2L19	10:33	Larkhall	Milngavie
2C30	11:39	Milngavie	Cumbernauld
5F33	13:06	Cumbernauld	Cumbernauld
2F33	13:17	Cumbernauld	Dalmuir
2R02	15:03	Dalmuir	Motherwell
2F03	16:15	Motherwell	Dalmuir
2R12	17:33	Dalmuir	Whifflet
5S15	18:27	Whifflet	Whifflet
2S15	18:58	Whifflet	Dalmuir
5L12	19:56	Dalmuir	Dalmuir
2L12	20:19	Dalmuir	Larkhall
2L15	21:33	Larkhall	Milngavie
2C36	23:13	Milngavie	Motherwell
5C36	**00:06**	**Motherwell**	**Motherwell Weighs C. H. S.**

No.318 250 (above) : *A close up of this EMU upon arrival at Larkhall.*

Milngavie

Side By Side (above) : *The train I arrived on from Larkhall sits at Platform 2 alongside Class 320 EMU No.320 417 standing at Platform 1, which had arrived at 09:35hrs from Larkhall.. This will now form 2C32, the 12:11 Milngavie - Motherwell. I had a mere five minute turnround before No.318 250 departed for Cumbernauld.*

One observation I would make, is that I was very impressed with how clean and tidy the stations I visited were; no litter and it would appear that station staff take pride in looking after their local station.

Onward and Westward

Milngavie

Milngavie station was reached, 3 miles and 16 chains after leaving the main line at Westerton Junction, the last mile or so being single track after leaving Hillfoot; the station is formed of two platforms. After leaving Milngavie, I would have to retrace my steps as far as Westerton in order to catch a train to the next location - Balloch.

The station is the usual access point for the 96 mile-long West Highland Way to Fort William, a long-distance trail which officially starts in Milngavie town centre, marked by a granite obelisk. The first few hundred yards follow a former spur of the railway originally built to serve the Ellangowan Paper Mills.

Interestingly, the town is a very popular retirement location, with an unusually high proportion of elderly residents; the 2001 census reported the town had a population of 12,795 in 5,256 households.

After leaving Milngavie, I made my way further west, still north of the River Clyde, to visit two more branches, Balloch and Helensburgh Central, via Westerton and Dalreoch.

Balloch

The station is a terminus on the North Clyde Line, 20 miles north west of Glasgow Queen Street and lies within the boundary (by just over 150 metres) of the Loch Lomond & Trossachs National Park and is the only example of an overhead electrified railway operating within any UK national park.

Balloch station was opened by British Rail in April 1988, replacing the former Balloch Central station which was situated immediately north of a level crossing on Balloch Road. The closure of this level crossing resulted in the closure of the previous terminus, Balloch Pier, in 1986. The present station is located 1/2 mile south of where Balloch Pier station once stood.

Westerton

(above) : *This is Westerton station, where I waited for my train to Balloch. It is seen arriving, formed of Class 320 EMUs No.320 305 + No.320 319, which is 2E71, the 11:16 Airdrie - Balloch.*

Balloch

(below) : *I arrived at the terminus station in the front car (No.320 305) of a two car set including No.320 319, which should have been the lead unit out on 2E54, the 12:37hrs service to Airdrie. However, for some unknown reason, this service left as ECS and I had to wait for another service. In this panoramic view of the station, No.320 319 waits to leave Balloch with, presumably, 5E54 ECS!*

Helensburgh Central

(above) : *Class 334 EMU No.334 010 sits at Platform 2 having arrived at the terminus with 2H01, the 11:50 Edinburgh - Helensburgh Central. My next move was to travel on the same unit to Hyndland (2H40), where I would change trains for a service to Cambuslang (2L12), thence a final train (2B86) to Lanark.*

Helensburgh Central (Scottish Gaelic: Baile Eilidh)

The station serves the town of Helensburgh on the north shore of the Firth of Clyde, which is a terminus on the North Clyde Line, 24 miles and 31 chains north west of Glasgow Queen Street; the western limit of electrification.

The station is Helensburgh's main railway station, the other being the much smaller Helensburgh Upper on the West Highland Line, which leaves the main line at Craigendoran Junction. Passing Craigendoran Junction en route, I recalled my time spent photographing Class 37s on West Highland passenger services in the 1980s and, particularly, seeing No.37011 pass the old signal box back in the 1980s working a passenger train from Oban to Glasgow Queen Street.

Helensburgh Central opened in 1858 as the terminus of the Glasgow, Dumbarton and Helensburgh Railway and ultimately the route became part of the London and North Eastern Railway under the 1923 Grouping. Responsibility fell to the Scottish Region on nationalisation in January 1948 .

The entire station building and platforms were rebuilt in 1897 to the design of James Carswell and today the station still boasts some fine glass and iron canopies; the station is Category B listed status.

Three of the four original platforms at the station remain in use, though the old engine shed and signal box have long closed, the latter in 1989, when the North Clyde network came under the control of Yoker signalling centre. The line from Craigendoran Junction had previously been singled in 1984.

Some readers may well remember when the line from Helensburgh Central to Glasgow Queen Street Low Level and on to Airdrie was electrified with the introduction of the revolutionary 'Blue Trains'. These British Rail Class 303 electric multiple units - 'Blue Trains' - ran on the North Clyde and the Cathcart Circle lines in Strathclyde and saw use for over 25 years, before being phased out finally in 2002, replaced by more modern Class 334 'Juniper' EMUs built between 1999-2000 by Alstom.

Lanark

Lanark is the county town of Lanarkshire. Lanark station opened in 1855, as the terminus of a short branch line off the Caledonian Railway's West Coast Main Line. The branch once had a triangular junction with the main line to allow trains from Lanark to head west towards Carluke or east to Carstairs.

In 1864, a line south from Lanark to Douglas was opened, extended to Muirkirk (Ayrshire) in 1874, where it formed an end-on junction with the Glasgow and South Western Railway. That line closed in 1964.

In 1974, as part of British Rail's 'Electric Scots' electrification project of the WCML between London Euston and Glasgow Central, the Lanark branch was included and electrified.

(above) : *"Journey's End" .....*

the last branch I visited on Thursday, 20th September 2018, was the one serving Lanark, which diverged from the WCML at Lanark Junction, 2 miles and 39 chains north west of Carstairs.

Class 318 No.318 258 waits at Lanark with 1B86, the 15:53hrs service to Glasgow Central.

Note the smart platform canopy and ornate ironwork.

(right) : *Station mural. This is depicted on the side of a station building and includes local landmarks along with the Coat of Arms of the Royal Burgh of Lanark.*

Thursday, 20th September 2018

320 306	Glasgow Central - Neilston	2N14, 08:02 Glasgow Central - Neilston
	Pollockshield East - Cathcart North and West Jcts - Neilston	
320 306	Neilston - Mount Florida	2N15, 08:43 Neilston - Glasgow Central
314204	Mount Florida - Glasgow Central	2N19, 09:05 Neilston - Glasgow Central
318 250	Glasgow Central - Larkhall	2L16, 09:18 Dalmuir - Larkhall
	Haughhead Jct - Larkhall	
318 250	Larkhall - Milngavie	2L19, 10:33 Larkhall - Milngavie
	Rutherglen Central Jct - Glasgow Central Low level - Finnieston East and West Jcts Westerton - Milngavie	
318 250	Milngavie - Westerton	2C30, 11:39 Milngavie - Cumbernauld
320 305	Westerton - Balloch	2E71, 11:16 Airdrie - Balloch
	Dalreoch - Balloch	
320 314	Balloch - Dalreoch	2E56, 13:07 Balloch - Airdrie
334 010	Dalreoch - Helensburgh Central	2H01, 11:50 Edinburgh - Helensburgh Central
	Craigendoran Jct - Helensburgh Central	
334 010	Helensburgh Central - Hyndland	2H40, 13:56 Helensburgh Central - Edinburgh
320 312	Hyndland - Cambuslang	2L12, 14:18 Dalmuir - Larkhall
	Finnieston West Jct - Kelvinhaugh Tunnel - Exhibition Centre	
318 258	Cambuslang - Lanark	2B86, 14:50 Glasgow Central - Lanark
	Lanark Jct - Lanark	
318 258	Lanark - Glasgow Central	2B87, 15:53 Lanark - Glasgow Central
320 307	Glasgow Central - King's Park	2P22, 17:11 Glasgow Central - Newton
	Cathcart North Jct - King's Park	
314 209	King's Park - Glasgow Central	2M91, 17:19 Newton - Glasgow Central

---

Notes on the branches:

Neilston	7 miles 46 chains	from Cathcart West Junction
Larkhall	3 miles 00 chains	from Haughhead Junction
Milngavie	3 miles 16 chains	from Westerton Junction
Balloch	4 miles 00 chains	from Dalreoch Junction
Helensburgh Central	1 mile 31 chains	from Craigendoran Junction
Lanark	2 miles 42 chains	from Lanark Junction

Day 4

The Final Day

I was really looking forward, even after a great couple of days, to some more new lines and the bonus of loco-hauled travel to finish my sojourn in Scotland.

The day was going to pan out like this:

1. **Alloa**   -   travel on a previous 'freight-only' line reinstated for passenger use.

2. **Tweedbank**   -   a new line built on part of the old 'Waverley Route'

3. **North Berwick** -   a trip to this outpost on the North Sea coast.

4. **'Fife Circle'**   -   DRS Class 68s on evening rush-hour commuter trains out of Edinburgh.

Alloa

I set out from Glasgow Queen Street on the 07:18hrs service from Alloa, some two hours before my Scottish Rover ticket officially allowed me travel (09:00hrs) - no railway staff seemed bothered about the early start and I wanted to enjoy as full-a-day as possible.

Alloa was 36 miles and 26 chains from GQSt and my journey would take 50 minutes to complete.

The line from Stirling to Alloa and further east was used as a freight route, ostensibly:

- MGR coal trains from Hunterston and Ravenstruther to Longannet power station.
- Aviation fuel tanks from Grangemouth to Linkswood.

After the closure of the Stirling-Alloa-Dunfermline line in 1968 and the Devon Valley Railway in 1973, the town had no passenger railway services. However, 40 years later, the Stirling-Alloa-Kincardine rail link project was completed in May 2008, after train crew route learning commenced in April 2008.

The line opened to the public on Monday, 19th May 2008.

Prior to this date, an official opening took place on 15 May 2008, where LNER Gresley K4 No.61994 'The Great Marquess' hauled four specials to Stirling. The return workings were hauled by 'Deltic' Class 55 No.55022 'Royal Scots Grey'.

Electrification : The project to electrify the line at 25kV 50Hz ac started in November 2016 and on 9th December 2018 ScotRail began operating electric services from Stirling to Alloa following completion of electrification - three months after my visit.

New Class 385 EMUs supplied by Hitachi Rail Europe took over Glasgow Queen Street – Stirling – Alloa services.

History

Originally, Alloa station was opened by the Stirling and Dunfermline Railway in August 1850 when the line was opened. Passengers for Stirling were transported via ferry along the River Forth to Stirling until the line to Stirling opened in July 1852, but the terminus was to the north of the Forth.

In July 1853, the bridge across the Forth was opened and the line extended to Stirling; subsequent links were added southwards to Larbert via the Alloa Railway in 1889 and northwards to Tillicoultry from 1851. In 1906, a second line to Dunfermline via Kincardine and Longannet opened along the northern bank of the Forth estuary, which had a passenger service until July 1930.

As built, Alloa station consisted of a wide island platform with two inset bays at its west end, for trains southwards to Larbert and Grangemouth and on the Alva branch line. The station was absorbed into the LNER during the Grouping of 1923, passing on to the Scottish Region of British Railways on nationalisation in 1948.

It was closed by the British Railways Board in 1968.

Alloa (above) : *Class 170 DMU No.170 455 is seen upon arrival at Alloa, having brought me there on 2N59, the 07:18hrs terminating service from Glasgow Queen St. As you can see, the OHLE is in place ready for the December switch on. I travelled back to GQSt on this DMU, thence a Class 334 EMU to Edinburgh.*

Note Milepost 7, which is the mileage from Stirling.

Glasgow Queen Street ------> Bishopbriggs ------> Greenhill Lower Jct ------> Carmuirs West Jct ------> Larbert	
Stirling ------> **Causewayhead Jct** ------> **Alloa**	**6 miles 62 chains**

"Onwards to Edinburgh"

Arriving at Edinburgh Waverley station - also known simply as Waverley - which is the principal station serving Edinburgh, the capital city of Scotland, and the second busiest station in Scotland, after Glasgow Central.

It is the northern terminus of the East Coast Main Line, 393 miles from London King's Cross, although some trains run through to Glasgow Central, Inverness and Aberdeen. Services to and from Edinburgh Waverley are primarily operated by ScotRail, including:

- five routes to Glasgow.
- the 'Fife Circle'
- the recently reopened Borders Railway
- services to Stirling / Dunblane / Alloa / North Berwick / Dunbar.

The station is also the terminus of the Edinburgh leg of the West Coast Main Line along with long distance inter-city 'cross country' trains to destinations such as Leeds, Sheffield, Derby, Birmingham New Street, Bristol Temple Meads and the west of England.

The station really has an international feel to it, plenty of amenities and loads of passengers with nationalities from all over the world.

Waverley station is situated in a steep, narrow valley between the medieval Old Town and the 18th century New Town and is named after Sir Walter Scott's Waverley novels.

EDINBURGH WAVERLEY

The main station facilities at Waverley are located in the middle of what is ostensibly a large island platform, surrounded by platforms on all four sides. There are 20 numbered platforms, three of which are three pairs of platforms which share the same tracks, so .....

a) Two tracks on the north side:

   The northernmost track is split between Platform 20 (west) and Platform 1 (east),
   the other is split between Platform 19 (west) and Platform 2 (east).

b) Four east-facing bay platforms, Platforms 3 to 6.

c) Four tracks on the south side, which are, from north to south:

   A track, which is split between Platform 11 (west) and Platform 7 (east).

   Platform 10.

   Platform 9, which is subdivided into "9w" (west) and "9e" (east) sections.

   Platform 8, which is subdivided likewise.

d) Seven west-facing bay platforms, Platforms 12 to 8.

During 2006 - 2007 parts of Waverley were modernised, including two new through platforms and the electrification of Platforms 12 to 18 in preparation for electric trains on the Airdrie - Bathgate route, plus other lines in Scotland to be electrified.

Between 2010 to 2012, the glazing of the station roof was entirely replaced with new strengthened clear glass panels, replacing the old 370,000 sq ft of mixed surfaces including felt, cloudy wired glass and plastic sheet. This has greatly increased the amount of natural light in the station, something to which I can readily testify.

Waverley Station (above) : *This is the view looking east from Platform 11 / 7 towards the partition wall, behind which are Platforms 8 and 9. Freightliner Class 90 No.90046 is seen stabled for use on Caledonian Sleeper services and, a At the far end of Platform 7, a Class 385 EMU waits to leave with a service to North Berwick.*

The 'New' Railway

The former 'Waverley Route' was a railway line that ran south for 98 miles from Edinburgh, through Midlothian and the Scottish Borders, to Carlisle, built by the North British Railway in two stages; Edinburgh to Hawick (opening in 1849) and the remainder to Carlisle, which opened in 1862.

The route chosen was to navigate a path around the formidable natural barriers south of Edinburgh in the form of the Southern Uplands and the summits at Whitrope (1,006ft) and Falahill (880ft). The landscape was such that these two areas of high ground could not be avoided and is one reason this route was considered to be the toughest main line in Britain due to its constant curves and continuous steep gradients.

For example, the southbound climb to Falahill was a stiff ruling gradient of 1 in 70 for some nine miles from Hawick, whilst the northbound ascent to Whitrope was 10 miles of 1 in 75 from Newcastleton.

The line was closed in 1969, as a result of the Beeching Report and it saddens me that I never had the opportunity to travel over it - until now, albeit only a part of it .....

The Borders Railway

After many years of campaigning to reopen part of the Waverley Route, in July 2005 the Waverley Railway Bill Committee supported a reopening as far as Galashiels. The Waverley Railway (Scotland) Act 2006 received Royal Assent on 24th June 2006 and sanctioned the construction of around 30 miles or so of new railway with seven new stations. The line actually runs for 35 miles and 34 chains to the end of line at Tweedbank.

Construction really started in April 2013 and involved building 42 new bridges, 95 refurbished bridges, two refurbished tunnels and the moving of 1.5 million tonnes of earth, not to mention new stations at Shawfair, Eskbank, Newtongrange, Gorebridge, Stow, Galashiels and Tweedbank.

In early 2015, work had been completed. On 13th May 2015, DRS Class 37 No.37604 with DBSO No.9702 worked over the line, running as 1Q13, Tweedbank - Millerhill test train.

Regular passenger services began on 6 September 2015 when the 08:45 Tweedbank - Edinburgh Waverley departed, formed of two-car ScotRail Class 158s led by No.158 701.

Going to Tweedbank

I was really excited at the prospect of going to Tweedbank for the first time and I was not to be disappointed.

It's a lovely line and the Borders countryside is beautiful; I kept thinking how great it would be if the line could be completed through to Carlisle, but that is probably just wishful thinking.

During the journey, I recalled black & white images in Roger Siviter's book entitled 'Waverley'; imagining Class A1 and A2 'Pacifics', working hard on the climb to Whitrope Summit, or passing Riccarton Junction - isolated and completely dependent on the railway for its survival.

The only blot on an otherwise super view through the carriage window was coming into Galashiels and the sight of a gaudy display hoarding for some large retailer - so out of character.

(left) : *The departure display on Platform 1 at Waverley station showing the details of my train to Tweedbank.*

Edinburgh Waverley (above) : Walking down *the platform, I could see Class 170 DMU No.170 405 waiting to depart with 2T76, the 10:54hrs service to Tweedbank, which I boarded for the 55-minute journey.*

Edinburgh Waverley ------> Craigentinny Jct ------> Portobello Jct ------> Niddrie North Jct ------> Brunstane ------> Newcraighall ------> Gorebridge ------> Galashiels ------> Tweenbank   31 miles 78 chains

Tweedbank (below) : *The end of the line, or the start of a journey, for No.170 405 at Tweedbank. On the other platform, Class 158 No.158 869 waits to return to Edinburgh. The station serves the village of Tweedbank, (population just over 2,000 at the last Census), Abbotsford House and Melrose. There is also a 'Park & Ride' facility at the station, to cater for the wider Scottish Borders community.*

North Berwick

After my return to Edinburgh, my next move was to go to North Berwick, a seaside town in East Lothian on the North Sea coast, a small terminus 22¼ miles from Edinburgh.

The town is reached by way of a single track line, which runs for four miles from Drem on the East Coast Main Line. There is little history to report, the station was built in the summer of 1850 by the North British Railway and the town was once regarded as a haven for the wealthy; North Berwick was often frequented in the mid-1800s by the rich and famous, including Albert Edward - the future King Edward VII.

In 1958, DMUs were introduced on North Berwick services with most branch trains running through to Edinburgh Waverley. The arrival of diesels, resulted in the closure of the engine shed. However, despite the improvement to passenger services, a period of decline had already begun. In the era of the infamous 'Beeching Axe', British Rail sought permission to close the branch line altogether, the Minister of Transport refused permission, but a drastic cut in service was implemented.

In 1985, costs savings were implemented. The grand old station buildings were demolished and the remaining platform was shortened. The 'new' station became unstaffed, and 'pay trains' were introduced between Edinburgh and North Berwick on 27th May 1985.

The line was electrified in the early 1990s by British Rail,at the same time as the 25 kV AC electrification of the East Coast Main Line. A regular electric service began on 8 July 1991. You may remember that during 2005, Edinburgh - North Berwick Line services were operated by English Welsh & Scottish Class 90s with former Virgin Mk 3 carriages and a Driving Van Trailer. In late 2005, five Class 322s were transferred from One to replace these.

In fact, from September 2018, ScotRail services on the North Berwick Line went over to new Hitachi-built Class 385 units, formed of six coaches (ie. two 3-car units). The former Class 380 units have been cascaded to Ayrshire and Inverclyde Lines to and from Glasgow Central.

North Berwick (above) : *As I departed from Edinburgh Waverley, the heavens opened and it poured with rain all the way to North Berwick, relenting slightly upon my arrival. Class 385 No.380 006 is seen having arrived with 2Y04, the 13:43 from Edinburgh. It will return to the Scottish Capital with service 2Y05 at 14;29hrs.*

Back in Edinburgh, I had just over two hours to kill before the main highlight of the day, DRS Class 68 haulage on the 'Fife Circle' commuter trains. During this hiatus, I took the opportunity to have a good look around Waverley station and the famous Princes Street, hence some of the images on Page 120.

Class 385 EMUs

(right) : *I must confess, I don't think these EMUs have any pleasing aesthetic appeal, especially with the cumbersome-looking connecting door at the front.*

Despite some initial teething problems when the 385s were first introduced from July 2018, by the end of 2019 all 70 units were in service.

These EMUs now operate on the recently electrified Croy, Dunblane and Shotts lines , plus:

- *Carstairs*
- *Cathcart Circle Lines*
- *Inverclyde Line*
- *Glasgow Central to Lanark.*

Their introduction has allowed ScotRail to cascade Class 156s, 158s, 170s and 314s to other areas.

In this view, Class 385 No.385 006 waits to depart from Platform 7 with 2YO4, the 13:43 Edinburgh - North Berwick.

North Berwick (below) : *This is the station sign adjacent to the railway station at North Berwick.*
Note, the model train.

Drem -----> North Berwick   **3 miles 30 chains**

Edinburgh Curios

"Skirl of the Pipes" (left) : *Looking very smart in all his tartan finery, bagpipes at the ready, a piper waits to pipe in the 'Royal Scotsman' charter as part of the luxury train's tour of Scotland.*

North British Hotel (bottom left) : *This famous hotel is adjacent to Waverley station at the corner of Princes Street and North Bridge.*

It opened in 1902, but sold by British Rail in 1983 to the Forte hotel group. Five years later, Forte closed the hotel for a year to extensively remodel and update the interior. It was renamed The New Balmoral Hotel, interestingly maintaining the "NB" initials!

On the skyline, is The National Monument of Scotland which is Scotland's national memorial to the Scottish soldiers and sailors who died fighting in the Napoleonic Wars.

Work started on its construction in 1822, but was never finished; the intention being to imitate the Parthenon in Athens, Greece.

The Scott memorial (below) : *This is a Victorian Gothic monument dedicated to Sir Walter Scott and is the second largest monument to a writer in the world, after the José Martí monument in Havana. It stands in Princes Street Gardens, opposite Jenners department store on Princes Street, which is also in this view.*

The 'Fife Circle'

What Is It?

This is the local rail service north from Edinburgh, linking towns of south Fife and the coastal towns along the Firth of Forth before heading back to Edinburgh. From an operational perspective, it's not really a circle, rather a point to point service that reverses at the Edinburgh end. If there is a loop, it is Inverkeithing to Inverkeithing. ie:

Inverkeithing - Dunfermline - Cowdenbeath - Cardenden - Glenrothes -

Kirkcaldy - Kinghorn - Burntisland - Aberdour - Dalgety Bay - Inverkeithing

Loco-hauled

Due to a shortage of DMUs, First ScotRail began running two peak-time loco-hauled services on the Fife Circle from 14th December 2008, one in the morning and the second in the evening. The train was worked by a DB Schenker Class 67 loco hauling six maroon-liveried Mk2 air conditioned coaches and routed Edinburgh - Kikcaldy - Dunfermline - Edinburgh, thus eliminating a top 'n' tail operation. The diagram was:

2K01, the 06:32 Edinburgh Waverley - Edinburgh Waverley

2G13, the 17:08 Edinburgh Waverley - Edinburgh Waverley

The 68s Arrive

From April 2015, Direct Rail Services (DRS) took over the operation of the Fife Circle commuter trains from DBS using Class 68 traction and two sets of six Mk2 vehicles, eventually liveried in ScotRail colours. At the time of my visit, these were the two diagrams:

Diagram 1

5K18,	05:11	Motherwell TMD - Cardenden	ECS
2K18,	**07:35**	**Cardenden - Edinburgh**	via Dunfermline
5K19,	08:47	Edinburgh Waverley - Motherwell TMD	ECS
5G13,	14:54	Motherwell TMD - Edinburgh	ECS
2G13,	**17:08**	**Edinburgh Waverley to - Glenrothes with Thornton**	via Dunfermline
2K14,	**18:15**	**Glenrothes with Thornton - Edinburgh Waverley**	via Kirkcaldy
5K14,	19:47	Edinburgh Waverley - Motherwell TMD	ECS

Diagram 2

5K03,	04:52	Motherwell TMD - Edinburgh Waverley	ECS
2K01,	**06:37**	**Edinburgh Waverley - Glenrothes with Thornton**	
2K02,	**07:46**	**Glenrothes with Thornton - Edinburgh Waverley**	
5G02,	09:00	Edinburgh Waverley - Motherwell TMD	ECS
5L69,	16:03	Motherwell TMD - Edinburgh Waverley	ECS
2L69,	**17:20**	**Edinburgh Waverley to Cardenden**	via Dunfermline
5L70,	18:24	Cardenden - Motherwell TMD	ECS

EDINBURGH WAVERLEY

(above) : I waited patiently at the end of Platform 2 for the arrival of the first Fife Circle loco-hauled set, to capture it exiting from the west portal of Calton Tunnel, and I was not to be disappointed. The ECS (5G13) emerged into the daylight headed by DRS Class 68 No.68006 and this would form 2G13 to Glenrothes with Thornton.

(below) : The front cab of No.68006 'Daring' pokes out into the sunshine, light streams through the station roof, whilst the remaining areas are cast in shade. Nevertheless, the 68 looks splendid, its 3,750hp Caterpillar engine gently purring away, ready to explode into action at the off.

This is what I had been looking forward to all week and I sat in the front coach with quite a few other enthusiasts waiting for the "RA" (Right Away) to be given by the station staff for train 2G13 to leave for Glenrothes.

'A Slip Up?"

The explosion of sound as No.68006 left Edinburgh and entered Mound Tunnel was deafening, yet exhilarating at the same time. After picking up passengers at Haymarket and South Gyle, it was full speed ahead and 15-minutes later we were crossing the Firth of Forth; I have included two views for your perusal, overleaf.

Before I knew it, my train came to a stop at Inverkeithing, where I alighted to wait for the second evening commuter train (2L69 to Cardenden). However, as I wanted to get back to Glasgow at a reasonable hour for dinner, I only went as far as Dunfermline Town, just 20 chains shy of four miles.

I decided to check my records and found to my astonishment, I had not set foot on Inverkeithing station for 40 years; the first time was on 6th September 1980, when I arrived behind Class 40 No.40151 on 1G64, the 12:40 Aberdeen - Edinburgh, alighting here to change trains.

This image (right) shows the 'whistler' waiting at Arbroath with some kind person holding the door open, so I would not miss it after taking my photograph.

Alighting this time at Inverkeithing may have been a mistake .... by not staying with No.68006, I did not complete the full circle: Edinburgh - Glenrothes - Edinburgh, which meant I still needed the 'south curve', amounting to a mere 42 chains (about half-a-mile), linking Glenrothes to Thornton South Junction on the Edinburgh - Dundee main line.

I had planned to do one diagram (2G13 & 2K14) on the Thursday and 2L69 on Friday, but the debacle of 'Storm Ali' on Tuesday meant this plan did not come to fruition. The only consolation was that I did travel on both 2G13 and 2L69, albeit in only short leaps.

So, there was nothing to do, just return to Scotland one year later, complete the Fife Circle route, and enjoy some more Class 68 haulage - not a bad prospect, I suppose!

(above) : *This is the view looking south from the footbridge at Inverkeithing where, due to the low sunshine, the station is cast in shadow. No.68007 'Valiant' slows for the station stop with 2L69, the 17:20 Edinburgh Waverley - Cardenden. The train will diverge on to the line for Dunfermline and Cardenden, 9 chains north of the station at Inverkeithing Central Junction.*

(Selective Images)

Dunfermline Town (above) : *This was as far as I travelled with No.68007 on 2G69, the 17:44 Edinburgh - Cardenden service, a measly three and three quarter miles!*

This station was opened by the Dunfermline and Queensferry Railway in November 1877, named Dunfermline, Comely Park. From 1890, the station was known as 'Dunfermline Lower', as there was 'Dunfermline Upper' station on the line to Stirling. After the latter station closed in 1968, the suffix was dropped.

In 2000, a new station was opened in the eastern suburbs of Dunfermline and given the name 'Dunfermline Queen Margaret', after the nearby hospital; to avoid confusion, the existing station was renamed Dunfermline Town.

(Previously)

The Firth of Forth

(page 124) : This image is the first of several I took looking through the carriage window on my outward journey with No.68006 on 2G13 to Glenrothes with Thornton. The Forth Road Bridge (nearest the camera) opened in 1964 and at the time was the longest suspension bridge in the world outside the United States; the total length is 8,241ft and the central span is 3,301ft long. The other, newer 'Queensferry Crossing', is a three-tower cable-stayed bridge, with an overall length of 1.7 miles, which opened in August 2017 and now carries the M90 Motorway.

(page 125) : Tanker berths lie off Hound Point, which is a rocky headland on the southern shore, opening in 1975, owned and operated by Ineos as an oil-export terminal for North Sea oil. The terminal is made up of two sea-island berths that can load tankers of up to 350,000 tonnes Dead weight. In this view, the crude oil tanker MV. 'New Renown' is seen berthed at the terminal, built by HDW Kiel in Germany.

(left) : My 'Spirit of Scotland' 4 from 8 day Rover ticket.

Friday, 21st September 2018

170 455	Glasgow Queen St - Alloa Stirling - Alloa	2N59, 07:18, Glasgow Queen St - Alloa
170 455	Alloa - Glasgow Queen St.	2N52, 08:41 Alloa - Glasgow Queen St
334 015	Glasgow Queen St - Edinburgh Sunnyside Jct - Bathgate - Newbridge Jct	2H44, 08:54 Glasgow Queen St - Edinburgh
170 405	Edinburgh - Tweedbank Portobello Jct - Tweedbank	2T76, 10:54 Edinburgh - Tweedbank
170 405	Tweedbank - Edinburgh	2T77, 11:59 Tweedbank - Edinburgh
385 006	Edinburgh - North Berwick Drem Jct - North Berwick	2Y04, 13:43 Edinburgh - North Berwick
385 007	North Berwick - Edinburgh	2Y05, 14:29 North Berwick - Edinburgh
68006	Edinburgh - Inverkeithing	2G13, 17:08 Edinburgh - Glenrothes
68007	Inverkeithing - Dunfermline Town	2G69, 17:19 Edinburgh - Cardenden
170 xxx	Dunfermline Town - Edinburgh	2G10, 17:44 Glenrothes - Edinburgh
365 525	Edinburgh - Glasgow Queen St	1R11, 18:45 Edinburgh - Glasgow Queen St

"Journey's End" (above) : *Train 1R11, the 18:45 hrs service from Edinburgh has arrived at Glasgow Queen Street, the last service on which I travelled during my stay in Scotland. No.365 525 was the only EMU of this Class that I actually sampled during my four days North of the Border and the only one not in ScotRail blue livery.*

The next day, I set off for home on 1V62, the 09:00 Glasgow Central - Penzance 'Voyager', as far as Cheltenham Spa, where I would change trains for the final leg to Swindon. At least I had the comfort of a First Class seat on the four-unit Voyager, having space to stretch my legs.

(iPhone 7+)

9th September 2019

"A Long Way Home"

As I mentioned earlier, when I made my visit to Scotland in September 2018, I had not been able to:

1) Complete an 'out & back' trip with a Class 68 on the complete 'Fife Circle'.

   Not essential, but something I wanted to do.

2) Traverse the missing 'South' curve on the Fife Circle:

   Thornton West Junction to Thornton South junction.

So, I set off from Swindon on 9th September 2019 for Edinburgh.

As it was a long journey and the prospect of a four-car Voyager from Cheltenham Spa, I decided to travel First Class for comfort and extra leg room. Sandwiches, hot and cold drinks, plus a hot meal was also included in the price - breast of chicken in a hot creamy mushroom sauce, which proved very acceptable.

Upon arrival in Edinburgh, I had a good two hours to kill before my train to Glenrothes with Thornton at 17:11hrs, so I took myself off to Princes Street to see the sights, making sure I was back in time to see the loco and coaches arrive ECS from Motherwell.

No.68006

Edinburgh Waverley ------> Haymarket ------> South Gyle ------> Dalmeny ------> Forth Rail Bridge ------>

Inverkeithing ------> Dunfermline Town ------> Cowdenbeath ------> Cardenden------> **Glenrothes**

Glenrothes ------> **Thornton South Jct.** ------> Kirkcaldy ------> Burntisland ------> Inverkeithing ------>

Forth Rail Bridge ------> Dalmeny ------> South Gyle ------> Haymarket ------> **Edinburgh Waverley**

0 miles 46 chains

The day was successful and, as ever, the ride over the Firth of Forth a memorable experience, something which all rail lovers should do at least once. The vista through the carriage window is never quite the same, probably due to seasonal variations in the weather, although there is usually an oil tanker to be seen berthed at a jetty in the Forth.

As the train left Dunfermline town, the limit of my previous visit, No.68006 continued along the 'Cowdenbeath Line' and the remaining 18-miles to Glenrothes with Thornton. After leaving Cardenden, I started to look out for any signs of the old Thornton Yard complex, which was used to marshal coal trains serving the Fife Coalfield.

There were no signs left, but I thought I would look back in my records and see when I last visited Thornton Yard, which was 11th April 1976 and the following locos were noted:

        Class 08 : 08341
        Class 20 : 20218   20219 20221   20222   20223
        Class 40 : 40060

At precisely 18:22hrs, No.68006 departed Glenrothes and completed the little bit of new track I needed to join the main Dundee - Edinburgh main line at Thornton South Junction - mission accomplished.

In reality, the 'Fife Circle' is formed by a line from Inverkeithing via Cowdenbeath through the old Fife coalfield that loops round to Kirkcaldy and back to Inverkeithing, 36 miles and 20 chains later.

The train details for No.68006 'Daring' are:

2G13, Edinburgh - Glenrothes :   31 miles and 58 chains.

2K14, Glenrothes - Edinburgh :   30 miles and 66 chains.

(above) : *Here it comes, Class 68 No.68006 'Daring' pulls into Waverley station with 5G13, the 14:54 Motherwell TMD - Edinburgh ECS, which will form 2G13, the 17:11 Edinburgh Waverley - Glenrothes with Thornton via Dunfermline. This would probably be my final trip out of Edinburgh with one of these loco-hauled services, as they will soon finish, when more units and displaced HSTs from the Great Western become available.*

(below) : *The end of the first leg of my journey and No.68006 'Daring' stands at Glenrothes after arriving with 2G13 fro Edinburgh. A couple of other enthusiasts look on in anticipation of the run back to Edinburgh.*   (iPhone 7+)

BATTLE OF BRITAIN MEMORIAL FLIGHT

Before I left Edinburgh for my journey round the 'Fife Circle' with No.68006, I was fortunate to see the arrival of 1S15, the 11:30hrs service from London King's Cross, led by No.91110. This was the first time I had seen this loco, which carries a special livery to commemorate the fallen heroes of the Royal Air Force and the Battle of Britain Memorial Flight.

The livery was unveiled at an event held at York on 2nd June 2012, when Class 91 No.91110 was named 'Battle of Britain Memorial Flight'; a flypast by a Spitfire, Hurricane and Lancaster bomber 'Phantom of the Ruhr' was also laid on at the ceremony. In my opinion, this livery must surely be regarded as one of the most striking and innovative of any seen to date. Perhaps, the accompanying images (taken on my iPphone 7+) will hopefully demonstrate.

No.91110 also carries a plaque in recognition of attaining a British loco speed record of 162mph, set on 17th September 1989, just south of Little Bytham during a test run on Stoke Bank.

BATTLE OF BRITAIN MEMORIAL FLIGHT

SPITFIRE HURRICANE LANCASTER DAKOTA

(above) : *The sky was dark and threatening on both the outward and return journey as I crossed the Firth of Forth, probably for the last time loco-hauled. In this view, as 2K14 made its approach, the three towers of the Queensferry Crossing stand out like yacht sails against a backdrop of rain-bearing clouds.*

(middle) : *I'm now back at Waverley station following the arrival of No.68006 'Daring' with 2K14, the 18:15hrs service from Glenrothes with Thornton. After a short while, the loco and stock will leave for servicing, running as 5K14, the 19:47 Edinburgh Waverley - Motherwell TMD ECS.*

(left) : *The next day, at 07:30am, GBRf Class 92 No.92023 is seen having been detached from a 'portion' of the 'Lowland Sleeper'.*

It will now run-round and take the ECS to Polmadie for servicing, which is a set of new Mark 5 rail carriages built by Spanish manufacturer CAF.

The 'Lowland Sleeper', runs from London Euston to Glasgow Central, the rear 8 carriages of which reverse at Carstairs and continue non-stop to Edinburgh Waverley.

10th September 2019

Before I left Swindon, I had decided that I wasn't going to go all the way to Scotland and back just for a small section of track. I wanted to include something else to justify the time and expense and chose to do so on the return journey. I plumped for two more pieces of track I required:

1) The Bishop Auckland branch from Darlington.

2) The Corby branch from Manton Junction to Glendon South Junction.

The latter was potentially more difficult as, except for a 'before dawn' service from Melton Mowbray to London, there was only one train a day that travelled over the entire length of the branch, that being:

      1P99, the 16:27 Derby - Kettering

I had bought individual tickets for each branch, plus a single ticket for each connecting service. It worked like this:

    1st Leg : Edinburgh - Darlington
    2nd Leg : Darlington - Bishop Auckland - Darlington
    3rd Leg : Darlington - Derby
    4th Leg : Derby - Kettering
    5th Leg : Kettering - Leicester
    6th Leg : Leicester - Birmingham New Street
    7th Leg : Birmingham New Street - Bristol Parkway
    8th Leg : Bristol Parkway - Swindon

A detailed timeline for the Home Journey is shown on page 141.

(above) : *It was a wet and gloomy start on the "Long Way Home" and No.43309 has just arrived at Waverley station from Craigentinny with 5E09, the ECS for 1E09, the 09:30 Edinburgh - London King's Cross, which I would take as far as Darlington. I was hoping for a Class 91 + Mk4 set on which, believe it or not, I had never travelled. However, with the advent of Azuma train sets, this was the last time I enjoyed an HST on the ECML.*

(right) : *A Class 67 is situated at strategic points along the East Coast Main Line, to act as 'Thunderbird' in the event of any passenger service failures.*

No.67005 'Queen's Messenger' was seen stabled in the Provincial Siding alongside Newcastle Central station to act as the Newcastle 'Thunderbird'.

Newcastle Central station is actually on quite a tight curve and in this view, you can see Platform 7/8 and the 'Up Slow' line.

NEWCASTLE

My train pulled into Newcastle Central station, the largest station on the East Coast Main Line between Edinburgh and London King's Cross, which comprises 12 platforms, five of which are bay platforms.The station also serves the Durham Coast Line to Sunderland, Hartlepool and Middlesbrough, the Tyne Valley Line to Hexham and Carlisle.

Whenever I am in Newcastle, I always remember my first vinyl album by the progressive rock group *'The Nice'*, whose legendary organist Keith Emerson composed the *'Five Bridges Suite'* about the city of Newcastle upon Tyne, released in the late 1960s. At the time there were five bridges spanning the River Tyne, but now there are seven. They are, from west to east:

A189 Redheugh Road Bridge

King Edward VII railway bridge

Queen Elizabeth II Metro Bridge

High Level Bridge

Swing Bridge

Tyne Bridge

Gateshead Millenium Bridge

(below) : *This is my view from the train, as it crosses King Edward VII rail Bridge. The blue structure nearest the camera is the Queen Elizabeth II Metro Bridge and, beyond, the top of the arched Tyne Bridge is partially visible. The Tyne Bridge is similar in design to the Sydney Harbour bridge.*

DARLINGTON

"Of historical importance" ....

the Stockton and Darlington Railway operated from 1825 to 1863 and became the first public railway in the world to use steam locos.

Its first line connected collieries near Shildon with Stockton-on-Tees and Darlington, opening on 27th September 1825 but, as the movement of coal to ships became so important, the line was extended to a new port and town at Middlesbrough.

Darlington station is now a Grade II listed building and dates from the 1880s with its impressive three-span overall roof and a broad island platform, designed by T.E. Harrison chief engineer and William Bell, the architect of the North Eastern Railway.

Darlington became a busy interchange on the East Coast route, with links to Richmond (opened 1846 / closed 1969), Barnard Castle (1862 / 1964) and Penrith (1862 / 1962), the Tees Valley Line to Bishop Auckland (1842) and Saltburn (1861).

(above) : *A panoramic view of Darlington station with its ornate three-span roof and two bay platforms (No.3 and No.2). Through passenger services to the north use Platform 4 on the left of the island platform, southbound services use Platform 1 on the right - only the outside lines are electrified.*

(inset) : *HST power car No.43306 leads 1E09 away from Darlington, after my arrival from Edinburgh. The next step for me is the branch line to Bishop Auckland.*

(overleaf) : *Under the impressive trainshed, Class 142 020 stands after bringing me back to Darlington in time for the next leg of my homeward jaunt to Derby and the Corby branch.*

The Bishop Auckland Branch

Bishop Auckland station, County Durham, is the western terminus of the Tees Valley Line (also known as the Bishop Line), west of Darlington. It used to run to Wearhead, a distance of 25 miles, built in the 19th century to carry limestone from Eastgate-in-Weardale, also passenger services to Weardale. Unfortunately, passenger services ceased in 1953, leaving only freight services to Eastgate until 1992.

At Bishops Auckland, there is a connection to the Weardale Heritage Railway at the nearby Bishop Auckland West railway station for trains towards Stanhope.

Darlington -----> North Road -----> Heighington -----> Newton Aycliffe -----> Shildon -----> Bishop Auckland

11 miles 23 chains

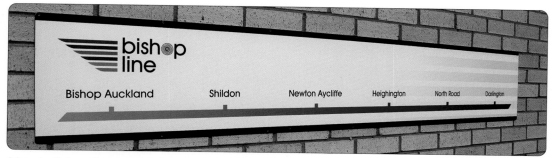

(above) : *Schematic representation of the 'Bishop Line' at Bishop Auckland station.*

(below) : *A delightful view of Bishop Auckland station showing the beautiful mural on the wall of the station building along with No.142 020 waiting to depart with 2D36, the 12:11 Bishop Auckland - Saltburn. The mural includes, among other delights, two famous men with association to the town:*

Comedian **Stan Laurel** *(Arthur Stanley Jefferson), who was actually born in Ulverston on 16th June 1890, son of Arthur Jefferson, a theatre manager from Bishop Auckland. Stan Laurel formed the double act with Oliver Hardy.*

The other gentleman is **Bob Hardisty** *(1921 - 1986), an English amateur footballer who represented Great Britain at the Olympics in 1948, 1952 and 1956, making a total of six appearances. Hardisty spent the majority of his career with Bishop Auckland, winning the Northern League seven times and the FA Amateur Cup three times between 1955 and 1957. He also made 6 appearances for Darlington between 1946 and 1949.*

Darlington - Derby

This was the second longest section of the journey home, at just 10 chains short of 145 miles. Unfortunately, the prospect of a loco-hauled service on the North East - South West route in the shape of a Class 45 / 46 'Peak' was long gone.

Today's form of transport would be a Class 222 'Voyager' unit, consisting of four cars.

Imagine for one moment, if you would, making the entire journey in Standard Class accommodation from Edinburgh to Plymouth .... it would, in my opinion, be like sitting in a dentist chair for 564 miles and some nine hours later your ordeal would be over.

A sobering thought but, purely from a comfort perspective, a seat in a Mk1/Mk2 coach in a 10-12 coach formation of a loco-hauled set is a much more appealing proposition - well, I certainly think so.

However, back to the task in hand ....

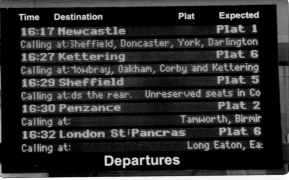

My train from Darlington arrived in Derby at half-past-three and so I had an hour to wait before my train.

There was not much to see, a few passenger services, but no freight.

I was pleased, and relieved I might add, to see that my train was displayed on the departure board as leaving for Kettering at 16:29hrs (via Corby) from Platform 6 as advertised - game on!

Time	Destination	Plat	Expected
16:17	Newcastle	Plat 1	
Calling at:	Sheffield, Doncaster, York, Darlington		
16:27	Kettering	Plat 6	
Calling at:	Mowbray, Oakham, Corby and Kettering		
16:29	Sheffield	Plat 5	
Calling at:	ds the rear. Unreserved seats in Co		
16:30	Penzance	Plat 2	
Calling at:			Tamworth, Birmir
16:32	London St/Pancras	Plat 6	
Calling at:			Long Eaton, Ea:

Departures

(above) : *Pulling into Platform 6, Derby, is 'Meridian' Class 222 No.222 017 with 5P99, the 16:04 Etches Park - Derby ECS, which will form my train - 1P99, the 16:27 Derby - Kettering. The station layout was remodelled during 2018, resulting in the original platform 5 (a bay platform at the south end) being removed and a new island platform constructed. The original Platform 6 became Platform 5 and the new island platform became Platforms 6 and 7, although No.7 is not used.*

(inset) : *The Derby station departure display showing my train for Kettering, via Corby.*

East Midlands Parkway : (above)

The 'Park & Ride' East Midlands Parkway is located near the village of Ratcliffe-on-Soar in Nottinghamshire, within easy reach of the A50, A453 and M1 Motorway.

The station is one mile south of Trent South Junction, close to the River Trent where the boundaries of Nottinghamshire, Derbyshire and Leicestershire meet.

The cooling towers of the adjacent Ratcliffe-on-Soar power station literally 'tower' over the station, which opened on 26th January 2009 and consists of four platforms. This was the view through the carriage window.

Oakham (right) : *This is a record shot of something railway related in Oakham, which is the only surviving passenger railway station in Rutland. As my train slowly pulled away from the station, I managed this shot of Oakham Level Crossing signal box.*

The station was opened by the Midland Railway in May 1848 and the signal box dates from 1899, constructed to a Midland Railway 2b design.

It is now Grade II listed and, interestingly for railway modellers, it achieved fame as the prototype for an Airfix plastic kit.

The Corby Branch
Manton Jct - Kettering North Jct

(right) : *This image, for the purpose of provenance, is taken through the carriage window, where 1P99 leaves the Oakham - Stamford main line, diverging on to the Corby branch. Manton Junction signal box is partially visible, dating from 1913.*

(middle) : *Corby station sign.*

(below) : *The current station at Corby opened in February 2009, replacing an earlier one dating from 1879, which closed in April 1966, but re-opened between 1987 - 1990.*

The line from Corby to the Midland Main Line at Kettering is now electrified and Corby now has direct passenger services serving London St. Pancras International.

Looking south, No.222 017 pauses at Corby, waiting for the road to Kettering.

Derby -----> Long Eaton -----> Trent South Jct. -----> Syston North Jct. -----> Syston East Jct. ------>		
Melton Mowbray ------> **Manton Jct.** ------> **Corby** ------ **Kettering North Jct.** ------> **Kettering**		
		16 miles 25 chains

Journey Miles	EDINBURGH			Mileage per Leg
	HST	Nos.43306 / 43239	1E09, 09:30 Edinburgh - London King's Cross	
160.43	DARLINGTON			160.43
	'Pacer'	No.142 020	2D19, 10:44 Saltburn - Bishop Auckland	
172.40	BISHOP AUCKLAND			11.77
	'Pacer'	No.142 020	2K14, 12:11 Bishop Auckland - Saltburn	
184.37	DARLINGTON			11.77
	'Voyager'	No.220 xxx	1V60, 11:06 Edinburgh - Plymouth	
329.27	DERBY			144.70
	'Meridian'	No.222 017	1P99, 16:27 Derby - Kettering	
389.20	CORBY			59.73
	'Meridian'	No.222 017	1P99, 16:27 Derby - Kettering	
396.59	KETTERING			7.39
	'Meridian'	No.222 017	1D57, 18:10 Kettering - Sheffield	
423.65	LEICESTER			27.06
	"Turbostar"	No.170 xxx	1N63, 17:01 Cambridge - Birmingham New St.	
463.49	BIRMINGHAM NEW STREET			40.64
	'Voyager'	No.222 xxx	1V68, 15:08 Edinburgh - Plymouth	
547.56	BRISTOL PARKWAY			84.07
	HST	Nos. ?	1L36, 20:22 Swansea - London Paddington	
581.95	SWINDON			34.39
M.Ch				M.Ch

Eastern Counties
Essex & Hertfordshire
17th August 2019

Background

Having completed a journey on the last lines needed in Norfolk and the northern part of the county of Essex back in August 2016, there remained a few branches left in Essex to do, along with some in Hertfordshire, namely:

Essex

Wickford Junction - Southend Victoria	12 miles 40 chains
Romford - Upminster	3 miles 30 chains
Upminster - West Thurrock Junction	6 miles 72 chains
Tilbury West Junction - Tilbury East Junction *	0 miles 26 chains

 * these junctions no longer exist, but once served Tilbury Riverside station, which closed in November 1992. I travelled to Tilbury Riverside in March 1983 using both lines of the triangle, but not the line directly between the two junctions, which is now effectively the main line.

Clapton Junction - Chingford	5 miles 75 chains

Hertfordshire

Bury Street Junction - Cheshunt	5 miles 18 chains
Broxbourne Junction - Hertford East	5 miles 64 chains

An Early Start

The good thing about this adventure was being able to complete the task in a single day, without the need for an overnight stay. However, due to prohibitive restrictions placed on travelling to London from Swindon on a weekday, I made the trip with my trusted travelling companion, Michael, on a Saturday. We could travel to London at any time and at a fraction of the weekday fare. With this in mind, I purchased a ticket for just £35.70, which included travel to and from Swindon, plus any six zones in and around London, inclusive of trains, buses and underground.

It was an HST (High Speed Train) from Swindon to London Paddington, thence the 'tube' to Liverpool Street station for the start of the day's proceedings.

London Liverpool Street

(left) : The signal box on the London underground at Liverpool Street is Grade II listed, but is now disused.

It opened in 1875 for what is now the Metropolitan and Circle lines' platform at Liverpool Street for the Metropolitan Railway's extension from Moorgate.

It was a non-standard design, built by McKenzie and Holland, of yellow stock brick with a weatherboard timber framed upper storey. It originally had a 40 lever frame, subsequently converted to an Interlocking Machine Room (IMR).

The 'box closed in November 1956 and operated remotely from the Farringdon signal box. Control transferred to Baker Street in March 2001 and, as of 2020, the IMR is still in use.

Leg 1 : Liverpool Street - Southend Victoria

The journey out of Liverpool Street was via the former Great Eastern route as far as Shenfield, where I leave the main line and follow the line to Wickford, from where a single line track leads to Southminster; a branch I visited in March 1983. Today, I continued my journey on what would be new track to the terminus at Southend Victoria, which is 41 miles and 42 chains out of Liverpool Street.

The line from Wickford to Southend opened in October 1889 and there used to be a goods yard to the east of the station, but this closed in June 1967. However, I did notice extensive carriage sidings:

- Down Carriage Sidings (North) : 10 roads, known as The Klondyke.
- Down Carriage Sidings (South) : 3 roads.
- Up Carriage Sidings (North) : 3 roads, known as The Shute.
- Up Carriage Sidings (South) : 2 roads.

Electrifying the line to Southend Victoria using overhead 1.5 kV DC current was completed in December 1956, changed to 6.25 kV AC in November 1960 and to 25 kV AC in January 1979.

After Southend, it was time to retrace my steps as far as Romford for the 2nd leg of the day.

No.321 422

London Liverpool Street ------> Romford ------> Shenfield ------> Wickford ------> Southend Victoria

4 miles 33 chains

~~~~~~~~~~~~~~~~~~~~~~~~~~~~~~~~~~~~~~~

Leg 2 : Romford - Upminster

This line is single-track throughout, electrified at 25 kV AC and attracts a maximum speed limit of 30 miles per hour. I noted that there were two trains per hour in each direction, operated by London Overground.

The line was originally built as a branch of the London, Tilbury and Southend Railway (LT&SR) and opened in June 1893 providing the LT&SR with a link to the Great Eastern Railway at Romford. From September 1956, a DMU replaced steam traction and in April 1957 a new bay platform (No.6), opened at Upminster, effectively making it part of the Great Eastern route.

There were (unsuccessful) attempts to close the line in the 1960s, but it was later electrified and EMUs began operating in April 1986. The branch is known colloquially as the "Romford Push and Pull" as it is single-track throughout.

Upminster is an interesting station as it shares platforms with main line train services to London Fenchurch Street station, plus London Underground; at the station there were two tube trains present which were going to work to Richmond and Ealing Broadway, respectively.

No.315 809

Romford ------> Emerson Park ------> Upminster   3 miles 30 chains

~~~~~~~~~~~~~~~~~~~~~~~~~~~~~~~~~~~~~~~

Leg 3 : Upminster - East Tilbury

There are two parts to this particular journey; the first being a ride over another single track line to West Thurrock Jct, near Grays, on the London, Tilbury and Southend Railway, followed by what can only be described as the shortest stretch I was ever likely to make - a mere 26 chains of track on the main line between the site of Tilbury West Junction and Tilbury East Junction, which once served Tilbury Riverside station. Tilbury Riverside along with the lines to the two junctions closed in 1992.

No.357 019

Upminster ------> Ockenden ------> West Thurrock Jct ------> Grays ------> Tilbury Town (Tilbury West Jct) ------> (Tilbury East Jct) ------> **East Tilbury**

7 miles 18 chains

From East Tilbury, it was back into London (via Barking) to do some more new lines.

SOUTHEND VICTORIA

(above) : *The station at Southend Victoria is formed of four platforms and Class 321 No.321 301 waits at Platform3 with 2K49, the 10:10 Southend Victoria - London Liverpool Street, on which I would travel as far as Romford. On the left of view is the 'Down' carriage sidings and site of the former Royal Mail Terminal. The 'Up' (south) carriage sidings are adjacent to Platform 4 on the right.*

(below) : *This is the view looking in the opposite direction, the decommissioned and boarded-up signal box and, in the distance, the 'Up' (north) carriage sidings.*

Romford

(above) : *Class 315 EMU No.315 809 waits in Platform 1 bay, ready to whisk me away on the next leg of my journey at 11:10hrs to Upminster (2V24), a mere 3 miles and 30 chains, taking 9 minutes to complete.*

Upminster

(below) : *On the far right, you can see No.315 809 at Platform 6, after my arrival from Romford. The station has two dedicated platforms (Nos. 4 and 5) for London Underground services, where 'S-Stock' No.21535 is working the District Line to Richmond while, alongside, No.21532 is working another District Line train service to Ealing Broadway. To the left, out of view, is the main line to London Fenchurch Street.*

Chingford

(above) : *Class 315 No.315 812 has arrived at Chingford after bringing me in to the station on 2T60, the 13:33hrs service from Liverpool Street, which will take me out of the town again at 14:10 hrs to Hackney Downs.*

(below) : *There are two sets of 5 lane sidings on the 'Down' side of the station, each facing each other, accessed from a single line connection. In the 'northern' sidings, three sets of EMUs were stabled which are, from left to right, Nos.317 709 / 317 729 and 317 723.*

Leg 4 : Liverpool Street - Chingford

I had already criss-crossed London many times in the past, but mostly on railtours and special charter trains, and there remained a few outstanding branches; one of which was the Chingford branch from Clapton Junction.

The station building at Chingford is relatively unchanged since its 1878 construction and still carries the grandeur associated with the railways in the late 19th century. The line was electrified by the Eastern Region of British Railways with EMUs starting service in November 1960, formed of Class 305s, later Class 302 and Class 304 EMUs.

Currently, London Overground operate passenger services and Chingford is one of three northern termini of the Lea Valley lines from London Liverpool Street; the other two being Enfield Town and Cheshunt.

No.315 812

London Liverpool Street ------> Bethnal Green ------> Hackney Downs ------> Clapton Jct ------> St James St Walthamstow Central -----> Chingford

5 miles 75 chains

After taking a couple of photographs to record my visit, it was back aboard EMU No.315 812 and a relatively short hop back down the branch and on to Hackney Downs (7 miles 35 chains) to change trains for a service to Cheshunt, before the final leg to Hertford East. In fact, the leg to Cheshunt was with the same EMU that worked to Chingford, No.315 812, which just goes to show how intensive the EMU diagrams are for trains in and out of Liverpool Street.

~~~~~~

Hackney Downs

(above) : *While I was waiting for my train to Cheshunt, Class 315 No.315 806 pulls into Platform 3 at Hackney Downs with 2U49, the 14:22 Enfield Town - London Liverpool Street. As you can see, the former signal box is situated at the north end of Platforms 2 and 3.*

Leg 5 : Hackney Downs - Cheshunt

Cheshunt is actually served by two lines out of Liverpool Street, which are used by different services:

London Liverpool St. to Hertford East / Cambridge / Stansted Airport

via - Bethnal Green - Hackney Downs - Coppermill Jct - Brimsdown - Cheshunt

London Liverpool St. to Cheshunt

via - Bethnal Green - Hackney Downs - Stoke Newington - White Hart Lane - Bury Street Jct - Southbury - Turkey Street - Cheshunt

I had previously travelled over the majority of both routes, probably some 40 years ago, which just left one section outstanding - *Bury Street Jct to Cheshunt* - and this was the bit I was going to do today

My starting point for this leg is Hackney Downs, an interesting station, served by both London Overground and National Rail services on the Lea Valley Lines and West Anglia Main Line. It is 2 miles 78 chains out from London Liverpool Street and has a direct passenger link to Hackney Central station on the North London Line.

The station was originally named Hackney Downs Junction until 1896. The running lines were electrified in the late 1950s with EMU operation from 21st November 1960 and the original 1872 signal box was replaced by a new one in May1960 (still in situ) on platforms 2 and 3. This signal box was decommissioned in May 2001 when signalling on the line was centralised at Liverpool Street.

No.315 812

Hackney Downs ------> Stoke Newington ------> Bury Street Jct ------> Turkey Street -----> Cheshunt

5 miles 18 chains

Cheshunt

(above) : *Class 315 EMU No.315 812 sits in the bay platform at Cheshunt after arriving with 2D40, the 14:45 London Liverpool Street - Cheshunt.*

(above) : *No.315 812 waits to return to London, while a 'Stansted Express' service, led by Class 317 No.317 660, accelerates through Cheshunt on the main line with 1B39, the 15:12 Stansted Airport - London Liverpool Street.*

The Class 315 EMUs were built by British Rail Engineering (BREL), York, in 1980 - 1981, the fifth and final variant of British Rail's 1972 standard design for suburban EMUs, which eventually encompassed 755 vehicles in Classes 313 / 314 / 315 / 507 and 508. As for the Class 317s, these were also constructed by BREL, York, in two batches, the first between 1981 - 1982 and the final batch, 1985 - 1987.

(below) : *In August 2002, signalling control at Cheshunt was transferred to the Liverpool Street Integrated Electronic Control Centre (IECC) and although the signal box officially closed in May 2003, it still remains in situ, albeit boarded up. The 'box can be seen in this view on the 'Up' side of the main running lines*

Leg 6 : Cheshunt - Hertford East

I left Cheshunt on the West Anglia main line on a service from Liverpool Street through to Hertford East and, at Broxbourne Junction, my train left the main line to take the branch line to Hertford East. My train was formed of two 4-car Class 317 EMUs, with No.317 654 leading and No.317 338 forming the second set, which lead out of Hertford east back to London.

The new piece of track was from *Broxbourne Junction to Hertford East*.

Hertford East railway station is the northern terminus of the Hertford East branch line off the West Anglia Main Line, 24 miles and 19 chains from Liverpool Street. It is one of two stations in Hertford, the other one being Hertford North on the Hertford Loop Line.

There are two platforms, although Platform 1 is only used during 'peak times'. The current station was designed by W. N. Ashbee, which opened by the Great Eastern Railway in February 1888 to replace a station further east, dating from when the branch line from Broxbourne opened in 1843.

The station is now a Grade II listed building and, perhaps more interestingly, the buffer stop lights on Platform 1 were listed separately; had I been aware of this fact at the time of my visit, I would have taken a photograph. However, I made do with a few images to record my visit and boarded the EMU (No.317 338) for the ride back to Liverpool Street station to conclude an excellent day's track bashing.

No.317 654

Broxbourne ------> Broxbourne Jct ------> Ware -----> Hertford East   **5 miles 64 chains**

Hertford East

(above) : Upon arrival at Hertford East, a few passengers walk towards the exit off 2O40, the 15:12 terminating service from London Liverpool Street. No.317 654 will now be at the rear of 2O43 back to London.

(opposite) : *This is the view off Platform 2, looking east and the way back to join the main line at Broxbourne Junction. Hertford East signal box was made redundant when signalling was centralised at Liverpool Street under 'WARM', an acronym adopted by railwaymen to describe the West Anglia Route Modernisation scheme. Unlike the 1960s signal box at Ware, which has now been demolished, for some reason Hertford East 'box stands derelict, unpainted, and is now considered an eyesore.*

~~~~~~~~~~~~~~~~~~~~~~~~~~~~~~~~~~~~~

Saturday, 17th August 2019

321 422	London Liv. St. - Southend Victoria	1K22, 08:55 London Liv. St. - Southend Victoria
	Wickford Jct - Southend Victoria	
321 301	Southend Victoria - Romford.	2K49, 10:10 Southend Victoria - London Liv. St
315 809	Romford - Upminster	2V24, 11:10 Romford - Upminster
	Romford - Upminster	
357 019	Upminster - East Tilbury	2D26, 11:23 London Fenchurch St - Shoeburyness
	Upminster - West Thurrock Jct	
	Tilbury West Jct - Tilbury East Jct	
357 313	East Tilbury - Barking	2D31, 11:44 Shoeburyness - London Fenchurch St
357 013	Barking - London Liv. St	9B21, 12:22 Shoeburyness - London Liv. St
315 812	London Liv. St - Chingford	2T60, 13:33 London Liv. St - Chingford
	Clapton Jct - Chingford	
315 812	Chingford - Hackney Downs	2T73, 14:10 Chingford - London Liv. St
315 812	Hackney Downs - Cheshunt	2D40, 14:45 London Liv. St - Cheshunt
	Bury Street Jct - Cheshunt	
317 654	Cheshunt - Hertford East	2O40, 15:12 London Liv. St - Hertford East
	Broxbourne Jct - Hertford East	
317 338	Hertford East - London Liv. St	2O43, 16:09 Hertford East - London Liv. St

Here is a brief record of some of the other branch lines and routes I have covered during the past few years.

Each image, except for Nos 5 and 12, cvshows the end of the line in question.

(1) Felixstowe : (04/15)

2R10, 09:58 Ipswich - Felixstowe

Class 153 : No.153 322

Required Mileage : 12 Miles 7 Chains
Westerfield Jct - Felixistowe

(2) Severn Beach : (05/15)

2K18, 11:11 Bristol TM - Severn Beach

Class 150 : No.150 926

Required Mileage : 2 Miles 73 Chains
Holesmouth Jct. - Severn Beach

The railway first reached Severn Beach in 1900, but only for goods traffic to Pilning. A platform was built beside the line by the GWR in 1922 with terminating passenger services from Bristol starting in May 1924. This was subsequently extended to Pilning in a loop back to Bristol via Patchway from July 1928.

Through services to Pilning ceased In November 1964.

(3) : 2nd Severn Crossing

After entering the single line track from Holesmouth Junction, the railway skirts the shore of the River Severn estuary and affords superb views of the Second Severn Crossing, which carries the M4 Motorway.

The bridge was opened by the Prince of Wales on 5th June 1996 and has a total length of 16,824ft.

(4) Maesteg (05/15)

2L53, 10:45 Cheltenham - Maesteg

Class 150 : No.150 251

Required Mileage : 7 Miles 79 Chains
Bridgend Lynfi Jct. - Maesteg

The line used to go north through the old Maesteg Castle Street railway station (opened in 1864), until closure with the withdrawal of passenger services in 1970; mineral traffic continued to several collieries in the area until November 1985.

(5) 'Jewellery Line' : (09/15)

2C50, 14:34 Worcester SH - Dorridge

Class 172 : No. ?

Required Mileage : 4 Miles 36 Chains

Smethwick Jct - Birmingham Moor St.

I used the above service to travel home to Swindon (via Birmingham) after visiting the autumn steam Gala at the Severn Valley Railway.

In this view, Class 68 No.68014 is seen after arriving at Birmingham Snow Hill with the 10:45hrs terminating service from London Marylebone.

(6) Merthyr Tydfil

2M22, 10:258 Barry Isl. - Merthyr Tydfil

Class 150 : 150 278

Required Mileage : 8 Miles 18 Chains

Abercynon - Merthyr Tydfil

A rebuild in 1996 saw the station reduced to its present single platform configuration, with retail outlets now occupying the rest of the old station site.

(7) Rhymney

2P61, 13:27 Rhymney - Penarth

Class 142 : No.142 010

Required Mileage : 10 Miles 4 Chains

Rhymney - Ystrad Mynach

I arrived at Rhymney after taking the bus across the 'Heads of the Valley' from Merthyr Tydfil. This saved time and avoided the need to reach Rhymney by way of Cardiff Central.

There are sidings to the west of the single platform which are used to stable DMUs overnight.

(8) Coryton

2C17, 10:34 Radyr - Coryton

Class 153 : No.153 312

Required Mileage : 2 Miles 42 Chains

Heath Jct. - Coryton

The station was opened by the Cardiff Railway in March 1911, as Coryton Halt. It was renamed Coryton Halt (Glam.) by the GWR in 1926 and relocated in 1931. The line beyond closed in 1952 and was proposed for closure under 'Beeching', but survived. It was renamed Coryton in May 1969.

(9) **Gunnislake**   (08/15)

2G79, 12:29 Plymouth - Gunnislake

Class 150 : No.150 265

Required Mileage : 11 Miles 57 Chains
ST. Budeaux Jct. - Gunnislake

Gunnislake railway station serves the village of Gunnislake in Cornwall, although it is nearer to the villages of Drakewalls and Albaston.

It is the northern terminus of the 'Tamar Valley Line' from Plymouth, becoming a terminus in November 1966 after the line onwards to Callington closed.

(10) **WIndsor & Eton**   (09/15)

2W15, 10:16 Slough - Windsor & Eton

Class 165 : No.165 118

Required Mileage : 2 Miles 63 Chains
Slough - Windsor & Eton

This station is one of two terminal stations serving Windsor, the other being Windsor & Eton Riverside served by South Western Railway.

In November 1968, Platforms 3 and 4 were taken out of use, followed by No.2 in September 1969, The remaining Platform 1 was truncated, twice, each time during a rebuild of the station.

(11) : A small part is still a railway station, most of the station building has been converted into a tourist-oriented shopping centre, called Windsor Royal Shopping.

(12) '**Robin Hood**' Line   (07/17)

2D18, 15:38 Worksop - Nottingham

Class 156 : No.156 401

Required Mileage : 28 Miles 55 Chains
Shireoaks East Jct. - Radford Jct.

The line re-opened to passengers in stages between 1993 and 1998 which, following the Beeching cuts of the 1960s, had become 'freight-only'.

I travelled over the line from Worksop to Nottingham on my way home after a visit to the North West of England. The image shows my train at Worksop.

(13) Aylesbury : (10/15)

Marylebone - Aylesbury Vale Parkway

Class 168 : No.?

Required Mileage : 33 Miles 57 Chains

Neasden South Jct. - Aylesbury

(via Harrow-on-the-Hill)

Between 2003 - 2017, Chiltern Railways reintroduced a 'Heritage' Class 121 DMU 'Bubble Car' on its Aylesbury - Princes Risborough shuttle service. From Aylesbury, I sampled No.121034 to Princes Risborough.

(14) Redditch (09/18)

2R39, 11: 41 Lichfield T. V. - Redditch

Class 323 : No.323 241

Required Mileage : 4 Miles 73 Chains

Barnt Green - Redditch

The line once ran south from Redditch to Ashchurch and Evesham. BR closed the line south of Alcester in Sept. 1962 after suspending passenger services to Evesham. Freight continued until 1964 when BR closed the whole line south of Redditch.

(15) Stratford-upon-Avon (08/19)

2D34, 12:27 Stourbridge Jct. - Stratford-upon-Avon

Class 172 : No.172 345

Required Mileage : 0 Miles 36 Chains

Hatton North Jct. - Hatton West Jct.

There were through services from Birmingham to Cheltenham until 1968. Passenger services south of Stratford disappeared in May 1969, when the service to Honeybourne, Evesham and Worcester Foregate Street was withdrawn. Freight ceased in 1976.

(16) St. Albans Abbey (09/19)

2F13, 09:46 Watford - St. Albans Abbey

Class 319 : No.319 433

Required Mileage : 6 Miles 45 Chains

Watford - St. Albans Abbey

St Albans Abbey was the first railway station in St Albans, built by the LNWR in 1858. It was, as it is now, a terminus.

Although the Midland Railway opened St Albans City in 1868, it was not until 1924 that 'Abbey' was added to the station's title to avoid confusion.

Background

'Crossrail' covered electrification of the former Great Western Main Line (GWML) line from Airport Junction to Maidenhead and, in March 2011, the government announced its intention to electrify the line between London and Cardiff together with the section linking Bristol Parkway and Bristol Temple Meads. The final portion from Cardiff to Swansea would follow.

Following delays and escalating costs, the Conservative government announced in July 2017 that electrification would only be completed as far as Thingley Junction, two miles west of Chippenham on the Swindon to Bristol Temple Meads section of the route. Although the level of Box Tunnel had been already lowered to cater for OHLE (Overhead Line Equipment), it was reported that OHLE would not be allowed through Sydney Gardens in Bath or under Brunel's trainshed at Bristol Temple Meads.

Furthermore, the Cardiff to Swansea section, plus Bristol Parkway to Temple Meads, and Didcot to Oxford were also postponed. Bi-mode trains would fill in the gaps pending completion of electrification. Electrification as far as Didcot Parkway was completed in December 2017, to Bristol Parkway and Newbury in December 2018 and finally to Cardiff in late 2019.

The Photographic Perspective

Electrification and the unsightly intrusion of over-engineered OHLE is now with us, not to mention the spread of palisade fencing by the lineside. Many railway photographers frequently comment on the restricted choice of very poor locations on a photographically ruined Great Western Main Line.

This maybe true and, whilst Swindon has also lost a good share of really good photographic locations, photographing 'under the wires' presents a new challenge.

In this portfolio, I have attempted to show locations, before and after electrification, but not where a location has been compromised by the intrusion of OHLE. So, there is a combination of scanned 35mm photographs and digital images depicting a variety of motive power and freight services in and around a 7-mile radius or so of Swindon railway station.

(above) : *'Under the wires' at Swindon .... Colas Class 70s, No.70808 + No.70803, double-head 6M50, Westbury VQ - Bescot VQ with an assortment of engineer's wagons; on this occasion, a single MXA and several MHAs and JNAs.*   *(iPhone 7+ 07/18)*

(opposite : *The view from Platform 3 at Swindon station looking east.*   *(iPhone 7+ 11/18)*

Swindon

Brinkworth - Royal Wootton Bassett

From Brinkworth (Callow Hill) to Wootton Bassett, the main line to South Wales runs along an embankment and afforded great shots of passing trains which, to a greater extent, has diminished with the advent of electrification, which a few images will hopefully illustrate. The best vantage point was where Callow Hill road bridge crosses the main line. The road in question is a bit of a 'rat run' for local traffic between the A3102 (Royal Wootton Bassett) and the B4042 (Brinkworth).

(above) : *On a dull day, looking west, from Callow Hill road bridge, EWS Class 66/0 No.66118 approaches with 6A10, Cardiff Tidal - Colnbrook loaded steel for the construction of Heathrow Terminal 5.* (10/04)

(opposite) : *Heading in the opposite direction, FHH Class 66/6 No.66613 hauls 6V55, Dagenham - Tower stone empties, formed of new MJA bogie bogie box wagons built 2003 - 2004 by Wagony Swidnica in Poland.*

(below) : *Moving into a field, close to where the main line comes off the embankment, 'cherry red' 'tug' No.60039 'Dove Holes' heads west with 6B33, the 13:05 Theale - Robeston discharged petroleum bogie tanks. The 'MURCO', as we refer to it, is a popular choice of train to follow, as it been the only freight through Swindon consistently booked for Class 60 traction over the years.* (05/16)

"The Embankment"

(above) : *The South Wales Main Line is carried along an embankment between the M4 overbridge (nr. Wootton Bassett Junction) and Callow Hill (Brinkworth) and there is a photograph of sorts from ground level. GBRf Class 66/7 No.66774 passes with 6V32, Tilbury - Trostre steel empties, formed of Cargowaggons. This was a lucky capture as shadow and heavy clouds were fast approaching, hence the cropped image.* (09/18)

(below) : *A little closer this time and DBC Class 60 No.60054 passes at a somewhat sedate pace with 6B33 to Robeston. Evidence of embankment strengthening work is clear to see - what a mess!* (10/18)

(bottom) : *This was a lucky capture - having seen the train approaching, I stopped on the hard shoulder of the M4 Motorway (near Royal Wootton Bassett) to photograph. Fastline Class 66/3 No. 66304 heads a rake of IIA bogie hoppers, which form 6M90, Avonmouth Bulk Import Terminal - Ratcliffe p.s. loaded coal.* (04/09)

WOOTTON BASSETT JUNCTION

Wootton Bassett Junction is now completely unrecognisable since OHLE went up.

The junction is where the lines from Bristol Temple Meads and South Wales meet, six miles west of Swindon station, and the site of Wootton Bassett railway station, which opened from 1841 to 1965. It replaced Wootton Bassett Road, about 2.5 miles to the east as the station serving Wootton Bassett.

For five days, week commencing 28th August 2006, the GWML was closed at Wootton Bassett Junction for engineering work to be carried out to remodel the junction as to allow accelerated times for trains travelling to South Wales.

(above) : *FHH Class 66/6 No.66622 leans into the curve having come from the Bristol direction with a rake of empty IOA 'Gondola' bogie ballast box wagons, running as 6U72, Westbury VQ - Stud Farm.*   (06/09)

The GLOUCESTER Line

The line from Swindon to Gloucester, via Kemble and Stroud, known affectionately as the 'Golden Valley' route, remains unelectrified and did not form any part of the GWML's plan for electrification. In fact, the only major upgrade the route has seen over the past few years was to convert from single to double track in 2014 between Swindon Loco Yard and Kemble, a distance just a few chains shy of 13 miles.

Bremhill : *Or, Bremell Sidings, as originally called, the site of an emergency supply for RAF Lyneham airbase. The view looking south towards Swindon is from a precarious position on the busy B4533 road bridge, a 'rat run' linking north west Swindon and Purton Stoke and Cricklade; only a single car can pass over the bridge at a time!*

(top) : In the days of single track, the daily 'Speedlink' trip (6B55, Swindon Cocklebury - Cardiff Tidal) approaches with some empty canvas-sided steel carriers and empty PCA cement tanks in the consist, hauled by two-tone grey Class 37/7 No.37711 which sports Railfreight metals sub sector chevron decals.   *(08/88)*

(above) : In the double track era, DBC 'tug' No.60066 passes a somewhat derelict-looking and overgown oil depot with empty BYA steel carriers, forming 6M53, Swindon Stores - Toton (for Boston Docks). If only the sun had decided to shine, but this train only runs on a Tuesday.   *(09/19)*

Collins Lane, Purton : *These two images are taken by the side of the line at Collins Lane AHBC level crossing, Purton, just over four miles out from Swindon station.*

(right) : *The NMT (Network Rail Measurement Train) is a regular visitor to this line and, looking south, the 'Yellow Banana', as it is often called, approaches the crossing with 1Q15, Swansea - Derby RT. The leading power car is No.43013 and No.43062 is on the rear.*

(middle) : *Looking in the opposite direction, quite an ensemble came into view, and the vehicles were not going to visit a heritage railway gala or the like, but to work.*

Class 67 No.67012 transported ex-works Class 90 electric loco No.90035 from Crewe to Swindon, for it to participate in pantograph testing on the now electrified GWML.

Running as 5Z24, the 11:11 Crewe Electric - Swindon Transfer, the full consist is: No.67012, No.90035, prototype HST liveried Mk 3 No.11074, DVT No. 82115 and No.67028 bringing up the rear. (11/19)

Moredon (above) : *Moving into the northern outskirts of Swindon, still on the Gloucester line, this is a view from the former B4553 road bridge at Moredon. This line sees no scheduled freight traffic, save for the bonus of a twice weekly flow of empty scrap wagons from Liverpool to Swindon EMR and a weekly train of imported steel from Boston Docks to Swindon Steel Terminal. In fact, it's the early bird that catches these, as they pass here around 06:30 - 07:00hrs in the morning! In superb early morning light, No.60044 approaches with loaded BYAs on the 6V15, Boston Docks - Swindon Stores, a journey that started from Boston some 12 hours earlier.* (07/19)

(above) : *All that remains of the former Great Western Railway works at Swindon is the shell, which now forms the highly successful Swindon Designer Outlet Village. On a bitterly cold day, the low winter sun casts longs shadows onto the loaded petroleum tanks being held in the 'Up Goods Loop' pending a path. The train, 6P82 Robeston - Colnbrook is being hauled by coal sector Class 60 No.60090 'Quinag'.*   (02/00)

(above) : : *Another long distance flow which used to run via the 'Golden Valley' route was 6V85, Milford West Sidings - Appleford, which brought flyash from Drax power station for disposal at the Oxfordshire landfill site. Luckily for me, it was running very late on this particular day and Class 66/0 No.66101 is seen coming off the Gloucester line with its train of tanks loaded onto FCA container flat wagons.*   (03/15)

SWINDON STATION

Swindon railway station is 77 miles and 23 chains from London Paddington and is over 300ft above sea level, making it the highest point on the GWML between London and Bristol. In fact, after leaving London, the line runs on a steady ruling gradient in the region of 1 in 1320 all the way to the Wiltshire town.

The station used to be an island platform and was often a bottleneck as passenger services vied for platform space - westbound trains used platform 3 and London bound platform 1. However, in 2003, this problem was eradicated by the opening of a new platform 4 on the south side of the running lines for Bristol and South Wales services. At the same time, the track layout changed so that the new platform acted as the 'Down Main' and one of the through lines was removed, leaving just one to act as the 'Up Main'.

(top) : "A real blast from the past" .... Class 37/7 No.37714 stands on the 'Down Goods' line with 4V60, Calvert - Bath/Bristol empty 'binliner', waiting for a path to follow behind the approaching HST away from Swindon.

(above) : The changes made to the layout at Swindon, including a new Platform 4, are clear for all to see, as DBC No.66024 and Colas No.66847 top 'n' tail 3S59, Barton Hill - Barton Hill RHTT service. The platform advertising hoarding for the Nationwide building society is quite fitting, as the Company's HQ is in Swindon.   (10/18)

(above) : *Swindon Steel Terminal, aka Swindon Stores, opened for business on 5th September 2007, ostensibly to handle steel traffic for the BMW car plant, which originated from either Llanwern or Boston Docks. I'm slightly perplexed about why such an ugly building was allowed to be built so close to Brunel's famous railway works.*

Class 60 No.60074 'Teenage Spirit' propels the loaded IHAs off 6C01 ex-Llanwern into the terminal.   *(03/11)*

(below) : *The daily 6M50, Westbury - Bescot departmental service can run with any consist or, as is often the case, light engine. Here, Colas Class 70 Nos.70812 + 70806 + 70801 pass through Swindon, running as 0M50.*   *(04/17)*

(above) : *When the 'Berks & Hants' route via Newbury is blocked for engineering work, freight services divert via Swindon. A very heavily laden 'Jumbo' stone train is double-headed by Class 59/2 locos, No.59205 and No.59206, which await the road at Swindon with 7A09, Merehead - Acton. Pathing a relatively slow train such as this on the busy high-speed GWML must prove a headache to the operating authorities.* (iPhone 7+ 08/18)

(below) : *It's an extremely wet and dull day, so typical of the weather during the winter of 2019/2020. The green colour light reflects in the puddles on the platform as Freightliner-operated low emission loco No.66956 pauses on the 'Up Main' with 4L36, Cardiff Wentloog - Felixstowe.* (02/20)

(above) : *The view looking west off Swindon station is now totally unrecognisable since the wires went up, a canopy of grey matter dominates the scene. In this view, a splash of colour is provided by Freightliner's Class 66/5 No.66587 in a striking corporate pink livery of 'ONE' (Ocean Network Express), as No.66587 'As One We Can' approaches on the 'Up Main' with 4L36, Cardiff Wentloog - Felixstowe freightliner.* (07/19)

(below) : *So many shades of grey .... a Class 166, No.166207, displaced from Thames Valley services following the introduction of Class 387 EMUs, approaches with a terminating service from Westbury. Meanwhile DBC Class 60 No.60091 awaits the road with 6B33, Theale - Robeston empty petroleum tanks.* (09/18)

(above) : In June 2002, a daily freightliner service was introduced between Cardiff and Southampton, booked for Class 57 traction, routed via Swindon and Reading to preserve route knowledge for Freightliner train crew. No.57003 'Freightliner Evolution' is seen passing with 4O51, Cardiff Wentloog - Southampton Millbrook and note the Class 180 unit leaving for Cardiff Central and a Plasser parked on the old stabling point.   (06/02)

(below) : Along with electrification, new MAS signalling was installed at Swindon station, as illustrated by Signal SW 1201. Looking west off the end of Platform 4, Class 66/5 No.66560 hauls failed No.66571 on another Cardiff Wentloog - Southampton freightliner.   (09/18)

(above) : *Clear and unobstructed open views were the order of the day before the wires went up.*

Two DRS (Direct Rail Services) 37s are seen working top 'n' tail, after a reversal in Cocklebury Yard, Swindon, with 1B00, the 12:00 Swindon - Swansea test train. The locos are No.37612 (leading) and No.37607 (rear). (07/06)

(middle) : *In this 'going away' shot, Colas Class 66/8 No.66850 leads sister No.66847 on 3S59, Barton Hill - Barton Hill, as they make their way along the 'Up Main' line. The signal 'feather' indicates the train will shortly cross over to the 'Down Main' line.*

(iPhone 7+ 11/18)

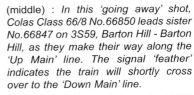

(left) : *Class 59/1 No.59101 'Village of Whatley' pulls out of Swindon East Loop after a short recess with 7C48, Appleford - Westbury yard stone empties.*

The loco carries Hanson Quarry Products livery of dark blue/silver with oxide red roof; note the stanchions on the left which will form part of the electrification training centre. (03/16)

(above/below) : ***"Awaiting a Path"*** .... Class 60 No.60091 'Barry Needham' sits in the 'Down/East Loop' with 6B33, Theale - Robeston discharged bogie tanks, ready to go after the HST on 1B46, London Paddington - Swansea clears the section.

Minutes later, No.60091 gets the road and slowly enters Platform 4 to continue its journey. Since then, 6B33 has been re-routed via Bedwyn and Westbury due to pathing difficulties on the GWML.   *(09/18)*

"Variety is the Spice of Life" ...... the movement of rolling stock for repair, storage and scrap is closely followed by enthusiasts, especially when these trains bring interesting motive power to railway lines not normally associated with such traction. Here is a small selection ......

(above) : DRS (Direct Rail Services) have been contracted to take Greater Anglia DVTs (Driver Van Trailer) to Cardiff Canton for remedial attention. On a drab day, befitting the external appearance of the Class 37/4 loco, No.37423 accelerates through Platform 4 at Swindon with 5Z37, Norwich Crown Point - Cardiff Canton. In the distance, the rear of 6C36, Moorswater - Aberthaw cement empties can be seen preparing to enter the 'Down' yard to reverse, having been diverted from Westbury due to engineering work. (iPhone 7+ 11/18)

(below) : There's 60 years spanning the IEP train at Platform 4 and the Class 37 standing on the 'Up Main', which was built in 1960. No.37402 'Stephen Middlemore' is returning to Norwich Crown Point light engine, as there was no payload with which to return with. This working is double-manned to avoid the necessity of making several stops on the way to change crew. (09/19)

(opposite) : Although this location is outside the boundary of this section, it's inclusion is merited because it was the very first 'scrapper' I photographed, At Denchworth, on the GWML, GBRf Class 66/7 No.667908 'Jayne' is in charge of 6V91, Shoeburyness - Newport Docks with three 'VEP' EMUs in tow; Nos.3586, 3412 and 3496. This was a time when all 'Slam-Door' EMUs were being withdrawn from service and sent for scrap. (09/05)

5Q76 (above) : *Class 20s on the GWML is certainly a rarity, in fact I can only remember one occasion, some 40 years ago when a pair worked into Swindon Cocklebury with the mid-day transfer freight from Gloucester. So the diagramming of a pair of 20s on this stock move was something not to be missed. Here, two Railfreight grey, large logo, Class 20s, No.20132 'Barrow Hill Depot' + No.20118 'Saltburn-by-the-Sea' approach the site of Ashbury Crossing with 5Q76, the 07:36 Ely Papworths - Newport Docks, taking Great Western Railway Mk3 HST vehicles for scrap.* (04/20)

(below) : Five days later, same place, same train, but this time the traction is another pair of Harry Needle 'choppers', in the form of the distinctly orange liveried Nos.20314 + 20311. (05/20)

5Z35 (above) : *What a smashing sight - a 'grid' working on the GWML, albeit pulling a single Chiltern Railways Mk 3 coach for refurbishment. Looking ex-works in former Railfreight colours of bodyside grey and yellow cabs, No.56104 heads west with 5Z35, Wembley - Barton Hill.* (02/16)

5Q78 (below) : *In 2019, Great Northern started to withdraw their fleet of Class 313 EMUs from service, despatching them to the Simsgroup in Newport for scrapping. Rail Operations Group Class 37/8 No.37884 'Cepheus', sporting Europhoenix livery, is seen at Marston Crossing with 5Q78, Hornsey - Newport Docks with Class 313 EMUs No.313051 + No.313039 in tow. Ex-No.37183, this loco was originally No.D6883, when built in November 1963.* (09/19)

5Z38 (above) : Resplendent in DRS Compass livery, No.37716 approaches Marston Crossing with 5Z38, the 08:42 Norwich Crown Point - Newport Docks taking some more former Greater Anglia vehicles for scrap. The consist is DVT No.82102, coaches No.10262 and No.12153, and DVTs numbered 82105, 82152, 82132 and 82103.   (05/20)

5Q32 (below) : Sets of Spanish built Mk 5 coaches for Trans Pennine loco hauled services have been imported into the UK via Portbury Dock. Rail Operations Group BR Blue Class 47 No.47812 passes through Swindon in charge of 5Q32, the 09:41 Portbury Automotive Terminal - Longsight ECS with asome TPE coaching stock.   (10/18)

5Z40 (above) : *Reminiscent of a time 40 years ago when Class 50 hauled passenger services were a regular sight on the GWML. In this view, it's loco and coaches, but not a scheduled passenger service, merely an ECS. Class 50 No.50008 'Thunderer' eases under Station Road bridge, Shrivenham, with 5Z40, the 09:06 Bristol Barton Hill - Wembley, returning six refurbished Chiltern Railways Mk 3 coaches to their home base.* (11/19)

5Q78 (below) : *Class 57/3 No.57301 'Goliath' is seen at Ashbury Crossing with 5Q78, the 10:19 Ilford EMUD - Newport Docks, conveying EMUs No.315858 + No.315814 for scrap. Note the variation in livery; the leading EMU is formerly belonging to Transport for London and the rear one to London Overground.* (11/19)

Cocklebury : *The sidings on the 'Up' side of the main line are used to stable locos, while the 'Down Goods' line (also known as Swindon East Loop) is frequently used to hold slow moving freight trains waiting a path in between IEPs (Intercity Express Programme) in the hands of Class 800 electro-diesel units and Class 801 EMUs.*

(above) : *Two-tone grey Class 60 No.60055 'Thomas Barnardo', with an EWS 'Beasties' logo stuck on the bodyside, proceeds along the 'Down Main' with a rake of empty PGA 2-axle stone hoppers. The train is 6C23, Hayes - East Usk (for Moreton on Lugg) and the PGAs have all now been withdrawn.*   *(04/07)*

(below) : *Looking over the palisade fencing and the ever increasing spread of lineside Buddlea, DBC Class 66/0 No.66100 'Armistice 100 1918 - 2018' waits in Cocklebury to depart with 6B52, Swindon Stores - Llanwern steel empties formed, as usual, of both BYAs and IHAs.*

The loco was named on the 9th November 2018 to commemorate the 100th anniversary of signing the armistice following the end of World War 1, two days after the loco received its 'Cherry Red' livery.   *(iPhone 7+ 11/19)*

(above) : *Low-emission Class 66/5 No.66599 passes Cocklebury with 4L38, the daily 09:32 Cardiff Wentloog - Felixstowe freightliner.* (11/19)

(below) : *A 'tug' on the Wootton Basset stone train is not an everyday occurrence and definitely worthy of a record shot. The driver has been given the road and No.60062 'Stainless Pioneer' eases its payload out of the loop with 7B12, Merehead - Wootton Bassett, having also effected a reverse in Swindon Transfer Sidings. (Iphone 7+ 10/18)*

HIGHWORTH JUNCTION : Sited one mile east of Swindon station, this is where the former Highworth branch left the main line serving Stratton, Hannington and Highworth. It opened in May 1883, closing to passengers in March 1953 and to freight in 1962. Today, only a short spur remains giving access to the busy EMR (European Metal Recycling) terminal, which processes scrap metal for trainload despatch to Aldwarke, Cardiff Tidal and Liverpool Gladstone Dock. Sidings are also still in situ, which once served the Austin Rover plant (now BMW).

There used to be a footbridge (known locally as the 'Monkey Bridge') over the line that pedestrians used as a short cut to get between Shrivenham Road and Gypsy Lane, which (in my opinion) gave the best unrestricted views of trains in both directions prior to the advent of OHLE. This bridge had to be removed as there was insufficient clearance for the catenary and a replacement bridge was erected with very high sides, which now hinders the view.

(above) : *In this view, the old, latticed, wrought iron footbridge is being dismantled in readiness for a new bridge to be constructed, close to where this image was taken. In fact, the new footbridge, combined with all the OHLE, is a far less appealing vantage point!*

DRS Class 37/6 No.37603 enters the 'Up Goods Loop' with 1Q13, Bristol Temple Meads - Didcot Network Rail test train; No.37612 brings up the rear, out of view.
(10/14)

(right) : *EWS Class 66s and HTA bogie coal hoppers started to replace the much liked Class 60s and iconic HAA 2-axle coal hopper on the Avonmouth - Didcot MGR coal service in the early 2000s.*

No.66080 passes Highworth Junction on the 'Up Main' with the mid-day 6A65, Avonmouth - Didcot ps loaded coal. (02/01)

(top left) : *Having already proved that Colas Rail could handle freight traffic in the 'Metals' sector, the Company extended their operations into South Wales in December 2010 with two trains of export steel from Llanwern to Dollands Moor (6O78 / 6O55 and 6V78 return empties), booked for Class 66/8 traction.*

On this particular occasion, the return 6V78 train, running as a special 6Z78, is seen approaching Highworth Junction double-headed by Nos.66844 + 66843. (04/11)

(bottom left) : *Freightliner's 'Powerhaul' Class 70 No.70003 sweeps past Highworth Junction with, 4O51, the 09:58 Cardiff - Southampton 'liner. In the background, a 'shed' is marshalling MBAs loaded with scrap metal for the evening's 6M73 service to Liverpool.* (02/11)

Highworth Junction (above) : An unrestricted view looking west, and what was probably 'working of the year' through Swindon in 2008. A pair of EWS Class 37s No.37406 'The Saltire Society' + No.37422 'Cardiff Canton' pile on the power as they pass Highworth Junction with 6M33, the 15:31 Avonmouth - Wembley 'Enterprise'. This train service came on stream in September 2002, starting out hauled by a Class 67 before becoming a solid Class 66/0 turn.   (08/08)

Highworth Junction (above) : A really colourful sight, Freightliner Class 66/6 No.66623 sports the new corporate livery of Genesee & Wyoming, an orange bodyside with two black horizontal stripes in the lower half and Freightliner branding in an orange, black and yellow logo. It is passing Highworth Junction with a Saturday STP working, running as 6V98, Hothfield - Stoke Gifford stone empties, formed of Freightliner Heavy Haul bogie limestone hoppers.
(07/19)

(above) : *The junction also gives access to the EMR scrap metal terminal on the former Highworth branch. No.66152 is seen propelling four MBA 'Monster' bogie box wagons loaded with scrap out of the branch and, due to length constraints at the terminal, a train loaded to 16 bogies will be made up in four separate portions. (05/09)*

(below) : *Recorded from the top of the new footbridge, the former DRS Class 66/4 No.66416 now in revised Freightliner (Powerhaul) livery of dark green with yellow ends and a grey stripe/buffer beam, approaches with 4V31, the London Gateway - Bristol freightliner.* (10/18)

(above) : *I managed to lean over the railing from the bottom step of the new footbridge to get this shot, which is probably as good as it gets! Due to engineering work on the 'Berks & Hants' line, freight services were being diverted via Swindon. DBC 'shed' No.66112 accelerates past the junction with the diverted 6M20, Whatley - St. Pancras stone, loaded in former RMC JGA bogie hoppers.* (10/18)

(below) : *Following the construction of a new waste management centre in Avonmouth, Greater London Council now send containerised waste to Avonmouth on a daily basis, plus one train from Northolt. Here, looking from the other side of the main line, No.66134 passes with 6C03, Southall Yard - Severnside SITA.* (09/18)

Stratton Green : Now that the GWML is electrified, the B4006 Station Road at Greenbridge, Stratton, does not really lend itself as a vantage point to photograph eastbound trains and, for this reason, I have not attempted to try for one. It is a pity, as this was an excellent vantage point before the wires went up.

Stratton Green is a timing point for freight services, as many will use the 'Up Goods Loop' to allow faster passenger services to overtake. The loop runs for 40 chains from Highworth Junction to Stratton Green.

(above) : *A pair of Freightliner Class 70s, No.70017 + No.70018 accelerate past Stratton Green where the loop joins the main line with 4O51, the Cardiff Wentloog - Southampton 'liner.*   *(07/13)*

(below) : *However, moving away from the road bridge, on to Stratton Road, I did manage this shot, albeit with the aid of some small steps leaning against the palisade fencing to see over - not recommended, I might add! Resplendent in DC Rail Freight grey livery, No.60046 'William Wilberforce' passes with 5Z20, Bristol Barton Hill - Wembley, conveying Chiltern Railways DVT No.82305, which looks to have received a fresh lick of paint and Chiltern Railways lettering applied to the bodyside. The 60 is substituting for failed 'Hoover' No.50008.*   *(02/20)*

South Marston Junction

This is where a spur links the 'Up Main' to Swindon Keypoint Railfreight Terminal, opened in October 2008. Despite a brief spell when Honda exported cars via Purfleet, the rail link has not seen use.

In fact, the junction was only good for 'Up' services, 'Down' trains into the terminal needed to run to Swindon, reverse, and retrace their steps on the 'Up Main' before propelling into the terminal - very inefficient!

(above) : *Colas Class 70 No.70805 passes South Marston Junction with 6M50, Westbury VQ - Bescot VQ consisting of two 'FDA' twin container flat wagons and some 'Autoballasters'. Apologies for the inferior quality of this image, which is a scan, as I deleted the original image in error.* (05/16)

Marston Crossing

Marston footbridge, near the village of South Marston three miles east of Swindon, opened in March 2018 and replaced a former foot crossing of the Great Western Main Line. The new bridge affords good views of the railway in both directions, which really only leads from one field to another!

(below) : *DBC Class 59/2 No.59201 approaches the monstrosity - sorry, I mean new footbridge - with the diverted 6V18, Allington - Whatley Quarry stone empties.* (iPhone 7+ 07/18)

"The Aggregate Score"

Marston Crossing is an excellent vantage point and here are some images to whet your appetite. On this page, a variety of aggregate traffic in terms of rolling stock and loco liveries.

(1) : *Looking over the footbridge parapet, Class 59/0 No.59001 'Yeoman Endeavour' approaches with the diverted 6C76, Acton - Whatley stone empties. The loco carries Aggregate Industries colours of green, light grey and blue.* (08/18)

(2) : *This is the first view of the daily 6B35, Hayes - Moreton on Lugg when it was operated by DBC. One of the ubiquitous 'sheds', No.66057, passes the same spot with a varied and colourful mix of empty hoppers.* (07/18)

(3) : *Looking in the opposite direction from ground level, Hanson-liveried Class 59/1 No.59102 'Village of Chantry' accelerates eastbound with the diverted 6A17, Whatley Quarry - Acton Yard. Upon arrival, the train will divide into two/three portions for onward movement to local terminals in and around London and the South East of England.* (07/18)

(4) : *Now under Freightliner Heavy Haul operation and booked Class 66/6 traction, train service 6B35 approaches with FHH 'HIA' empty bogie hoppers, hauled by No.66601, now bound for Moreton on Lugg.*

You will notice that the wagons come in two colours. When introduced in 2005 - 2006, they were intended to be used on separate limestone flows, but this seldom worked in practice. (09/19)

(above) : Reminiscent of the former Colas operated service, albeit serving Tilbury, this GBRf train of empty canvas-sided IHA steel carriers - 6V30, from Grain to Margam - is approaching Marston Crossing hauled by Class 66/7 No.66763 'Severn Valley railway'. Well over 80% of the 66/7 fleet have been named.   (08/18)

(below) : Prior to being placed in store, DBC Class 66/0 No.66008 transferred to GBRF in 2018. The loco is seen still wearing EWS maroon & gold livery at Marston Crossing heading a rake of empty IOA 'Gondola' bogie ballast wagons, running as 6M40, Westbury VQ - Stud Farm.   (07/18)

South Marston

After Marston Crossing, the GWML runs along an embankment, just south of South Marston, for two miles before reaching Bourton, the most part of which follows the A420 Swindon to Oxford main road. In fact, the section of line between Shrivenham and Highworth Junction is at a ruling gradient of 1 in 834.

(above) : *The view was better before electrification, but there is still a challenge to get reasonable shots 'under the wires'. This is a Saturday STP working, 6C03, Northolt - Severnside Sita containerised waste 'Binliner', seen on the embankment hauled by Class 66/0 No.66199. This vantage point is just off the A420 on the corner of Old Vicarage Lane, aided by a small step ladder to see over the hedge in the foreground.* (02/20)

(top left) : *This was a time when EWS were trialling pairs of Class 66/0s on heavy trains instead of a single Class 60 which, fortunately for rail enthusiasts, did not materialise. In this view, Nos.66194 + 66085 pass with 6B33, Theale - Robeston empty bogie tanks.* (04/10)

(bottom left) : *Roadside .... fortunately, no high-sided vehicles came along as GBRf Class 66/7 No.66713 'Forest City' on 6V43, MFO Angerstein - Cardiff Pengam passed me, formed of empty 'Bardon' JGA hoppers.* (04/15)

(below) : *Moving into a field near the junction of the A420 and Old Vicarage Lane, I was able to obtain a slightly different perspective of a westbound freight. No.60063 ambles along the main line with train service 6B33; a pretty solid turn for a Class 60 loco, which is just as well as they are otherwise a scarce commodity!* (02/19)

Bourton

The road bridge across the running lines leading to the village of Bourton (accessed off the A420 Swindon - Oxford Road) was a good vantage point to see trains in both directions, but this has all changed following electrification. Looking west, the lines are carried on a slight embankment, but in a cutting looking east.

(above) : *January 2015 heralded the start of several months of 'blockades' in the Reading area to allow for major remodelling work to be carried out. This resulted in the closure of the curve linking Reading West Junction and Oxford Road Junction. Freight services were diverted and car trains went via Salisbury, Westbury and Swindon.*

Here is the diverted 6M66, Southampton Western Docks - Garston service, conveying mostly small trucks on IPA 2-axle twin, single deck, car carriers passing Bourton, hauled by 'shed' No.66174. (04/15)

(below) : *Looking in the opposite direction, we see DRS Class 37/6 locos No.37612 and No.37609 top 'n' tail 1Z22, the 08:14 Tyseley - Bristol Temple Meads Network Rail measurement train.* (04/16)

SHRIVENHAM

A new and improved bridge over the railway on Station Road, Shrivenham, was opened in April 2016, the new structure higher to create additional space for the overhead lines. Combined with palisade fencing, there is just about a shot from the bridge looking east, or west from a field below.

The railway station was 3⁄4 mile south of the village, on the west side of Station Road (B4000), built in 1840.

In December 1964, BR withdrew passenger services from Shrivenham and all other intermediate stations between Didcot and Swindon. The station buildings were demolished in 1965 but remnants of the platforms survive.

(top right) : *"A sight for sore eyes" .... EWS 'tug' No.60049 approaches Station Road bridge with 6C64, the 11:59 Didcot ps - Avonmouth, formed of iconic HAA 2-axle wagons. (03/99)*

(middle) : *Looking west, Class 66/5 No.66566 runs past the old station platforms with 4L32, Bristol - Tilbury freightliner. (06/16)*

(below) : *From the bridge, this view is about as good as it gets. FHH 66/6 No.66613 approaches with 6B35, Hayes - Stoke Gifford. (11/19)*

Pre-electrification

(above) : *Looking over the parapet of the footbridge, the eye was greeted by a clean, open and unrestricted vista. In the early days of the Wentloog freightliner (4O50), traction was a Class 57/0, one of eight ex-Class 47s rebuilt between 1997-1999. In this view, it's No.57001 'Freightliner Pioneer', ex-No.47356.*   *(08/05)*

(opposite) : *The Avon 'Binliner' was a regular weekday runner until its demise in April 2011, the last loaded service ran on the 1st of that month. Before Freightliner took over the operation in 2001, this train was a good source of varied traction; 37s, 47s, 50s and 58s readily spring to mind. Passing Milepost 71, the all-green ensemble of loco and containers approaches the crossing with No.66616 in charge of 4V40, Calvert - Bristol.*   *(08/05)*

(below) : *An idyllic setting with bales of hay basking in the summer sunshine waiting to be collected by the farmer for winter feed storage. Cherry-red 'tug' No.60020 ambles merrily by with 6B33 empty bogie tanks.*   *(07/14)*

Ashbury Crossing

The level crossing on the Shrivenham to Ashbury road was closed in the 1970s as part of modernisation and resignalling to MAS (Multiple Aspect Signalling) and a concrete footbridge was provided, a few yards away from the original crossing. This bridge is solely a crossing for pedestrians and animals and has become one of the favourite photographic locations among enthusiasts and photographers in the Vale of White Horse.

Following modernisation of the GWML in the late 1960s, all level crossings between London Paddington and Bristol Temple Meads were removed except for two at Steventon; Stocks Lane (CCTV) and Causeway (MCB).

Ashbury Crossing has not deterred railway photographers since OHLE was erected, myself included. For this reason, I have included several images as testament to this claim!

Post electrification

Variation on a Theme

(above) : *Before going over to Colas operation, GBRf Class 66/7 No.66710 'Phil Packer BRIT' is seen heading 6M40, Westbury VQ - Stud Farm ballast empties. Taken from ground level, I stood on some concrete blocks at the end of the old road, so I could see over the fencing.*

Access to Ashbury Foot Crossing can be reached via Stainswick Lane, going south of Shrivenham, or from the lane off the B4000 Ashbury road on the other side of the running lines. (09/18)

(below) : *Viewed from beneath the footbridge, No.66766 is seen heading 6V32, Tilbury - Trostre, formed of empty Cargowaggons. If you view from the top of the footbridge, you will need a small step ladder to see over.* (09/18)

(above) : , No.66780 'The Cemex Express' puts in an appearance on 4V03, Tonbridge West Yard - Cardiff Docks, formed of both GBRf and Fastline-branded HYA bogie coal hoppers. The loco's livery dates from September 2018 and is a white bodyside with CEMEX and GBRf logos, plus red, white and blue bands over each cab end.

"Aggregates is the new coal". Following the virtual elimination of coal traffic in the UK, many coal wagons (eg.HAAs, HTAs and HYAs) have been scrapped or put to other use, as we see here.   (08/19)

(below) : The daily 6M50, Westbury VQ - Bescot VQ, this time under Colas responsibility, approaches with No.70807 hauling a rake of MRA bogie side tipping ballast wagons and IOA 'Gondolas'.   (02/18)

(above) : FHH Class 66/6 No.66621 approaches Ashbury Crossing with 6C96, Banbury Reservoir Sidings - Bristol East stone empties, with a smart set of new Freightliner bogie box wagons in tow. The effect of a low winter sun and the tall trees of Stainswick Wood behind me result in ever lengthening shadows at this time of year. (02/19)

"Before the Wires went Up" .... *DBC Class 60 No.60066 gingerly pulls out of Swindon East Loop and is about to pass through Platform 4 with 6B33, Theale - Robeston empty bogie tanks. The loco is adorned in silver with lower dark grey band and "Drax - Powering Tomorrow" branding.* *(03/15)*